THE MONSTER WITHIN

BRIAN GREENAWAY

CWR

Copyright © 2012 Brian Greenaway

Published 2012 by CWR, Waverley Abbey House, Waverley Lane, Farnham, Surrey GU9 8EP, UK. Registered Charity No. 294387. Registered Limited Company No. 1990308.

The right of Brian Greenaway to be identified as the author of this work has been asserted by him in accordance with the Copyright, Designs and Patents Act 1988.

See back of book for list of National Distributors.

Unless otherwise indicated, all Scripture references are from the Holy Bible: New International Version (NIV), copyright © 1973, 1978, 1984 by the International Bible Society. Other versions used: TLB: *The Living Bible* © 1971, 1994 Tyndale House Publishers.

Concept development, editing, design and production by CWR

Printed in Finland by Bookwell

ISBN: 978-1-85345-740-1

C✪NTENTS

INTRODUCTION

Many years ago when I was banged up in Dartmoor Prison serving a four-year sentence, I read a book that changed my life. It seemed to be written about me: a violent gang leader on a path to self-destruction, caused by the pain of rejection and mental abuse. But it was how this man's life was dramatically turned around that really spoke to me. I desperately wanted what he had.

I finally had the chance to do the same for others when my book *Hell's Angel* was released more than twenty-five years ago and now I have the opportunity to do the same again with this one, left as a legacy for those without hope.

I have been planning to write another book for about eight years now. Different friends had various ideas about what they thought I should write and I tried a few times, but it never felt right. It was only when I decided to write about emotional pain and rejection that I really felt that it was the kind of book God wanted me to write.

I believe that where and how we grow up leaves an indelible mark, rooted in our being, that can affect us our whole lives. We all face innocuous forms of rejection because making choices to accept one thing and reject another is part of daily life. Sometimes this can be personal rejection, such as being unsuccessful in a job interview, experiencing unrequited love or seeing your child not getting a place at their chosen school.

However, prolonged and consistent rejection – the dynamic and ongoing toxic experience of being perceived by others as being below standard and never good enough – is particularly destructive. Rejection by an entire group of people is even more painful, particularly when it results in social and familial isolation.

Such emotional abuse, as I have faced so many times, leads to a number of deep and adverse psychological consequences: loneliness, low self-esteem, aggression and chronic depression. It can also create feelings of insecurity, inhibits the development of resilience and promotes a heightened sensitivity.

I've worked for thirty-two years with guys in prison and I have heard my story so many times. When they say to me that I can't possibly know what it's like for them, I tell them that I do – I've been there, done that, got the T-shirt.

My work in prisons is coming to an end and I wanted to leave something behind for those behind bars to show how God has changed my life so dramatically. If it can happen for me, it can happen for them too. But this book is for hurting and rejected people wherever they are. They may not be physically locked up, but they are often trapped in their own mental and emotional prison because of what they are going through.

Writing this book was six months of agony as I relived everything I've been through and the awful things that I have done. But I know that God uses my pain to reach into the hearts and minds of people and help them in their healing. I certainly didn't do this so that everyone would think I am a wonderful guy; people often read a book and then put the author on a pedestal. I get really angry about that. I'm completely devoted to God, but I still get it wrong and make mistakes. It hurts when that happens and there's some stuff I've done that devastates me. However, I'm not a man-pleaser, I'm a God-pleaser, and I wanted this book to show my humanity and the things that I struggle with. And I still find it amazing that God can love someone like me.

He also loves you, no matter what you have done in your life. I want you to know, through reading this, that God is real and knows you completely, inside and out. He knows all the sin and He knows all the pain. He loves you and wants to be with you, in spite of anything you may have done.

To all those, like me, who have suffered years of pain and rejection, it is to you that I dedicate this book.

CHAPTER I

What did I do that was so wrong?

'Dad! I'm here, Dad! Why won't you say something to me? Why won't you even look at me?'

He was here again on our street, surrounded by a crowd of excited children. I stood watching close by – ignored, invisible and hurting so much.

Dad walked out when I was four years old, leaving me, my sister and my mum, who was pregnant with my younger sister. He returned almost every Saturday, but he didn't come to see us. He came to visit his sister living just two doors down.

Back then in the early 1950s, cars were a rare sight, especially in our small village. I used to look out for them, waving to the drivers as they drove past and writing down their number plates. Most looked friendly and waved back. But Dad never did. I knew roughly when he would arrive and sometimes I would wait inside, watching from behind our net curtains, but mostly I would sit outside with my feet in the gutter, drawing in the dust, desperate to see him. As soon as I saw his car, a large impressive black Ford, I would leap to my feet, jumping and waving energetically and frantically at him as he drove past, hoping that he would acknowledge me in some way. But he always passed by, face set straight ahead, ignoring me, and then he would turn his car around just past our house. By then other kids would be gathering in excitement at the sight of a car, and he would pull in outside my auntie's home. I would eagerly run to be with the other kids. As he got out, I would stand close to his car looking at the kids who were squawking around him. I would see him smile, maybe run his hand through the hair of one or two of them, making a mess of it, and they would grin at him as he walked into his sister's house. Not once did he ever even glance my way.

I've seen photos of my dad in recent years but I have no memory of what he looked like. What I do have, though, is the burning memory of crying inside, my heart aching every time this happened. I never said anything to him but in my mind I was pleading with him: 'Dad, please say something, please look at me and smile at me like you do with the other kids. Can you even see me? Can't you just give me one little booster, something to hold onto, like: "Hello son"?'

I waited for so long to hear that – most of my life, in fact – but it never came.

Finally I would turn around and walk slowly home, head hanging down, wondering yet again what I had done that was so wrong. It hurt so much that it felt as if someone had stuck a knife in my guts and twisted it. Mum would watch this scene and see how gutted I was. And every time, the same response was spat out at me: 'See, he doesn't give a monkey's about you. He's not interested. He doesn't care about any of you.' I was to face this bitterness and anger for the rest of my childhood.

I only remember my dad coming into the house once, trying to break in late one evening. I was always afraid of the dark and most nights I would lie in bed watching shadows on the walls, listening to the noises from outside, scared out of my wits. I used to try and lie as flat as I could so that it looked like I wasn't in the bed in case someone or something came to get me. And often as I was trying to sleep I would hear a horrible screeching sound, which frightened me even more. At some point later I realised it was just an owl in the trees outside.

On this night, I heard a scraping sound coming from downstairs and, scared as I was, my mum sent me down to investigate. It was my dad removing putty from around the window to try and break in. I unbolted the door and he burst through, grabbing my arm and twisting it up my back, making me scream in pain. I never found out why, but it forced my mum out of her bedroom. I don't really remember what happened after that. But I know that he never came back, leaving us with no support, struggling to survive and living with the stigma of being abandoned and fatherless.

At the time we lived in a village in Hampshire called Steep, about eighteen miles north of Portsmouth. We moved there when I was about four from the Isle of Wight where I was born and where some of my family still lived. Steep is close to the steepest and most contorted part of an escarpment in the hills, which gave the village its name. Surrounded by beautiful countryside and woodland, it is close to two very well-known private boarding schools – Bedales and the feeder prep school Dunhurst – and many large detached houses. It was very middle class and 'awfully nice' – if you had money, that is.

By contrast, we lived on the only council estate. Hayes Cottages was a row of just ten houses when we moved there, ours being second from the end. Extra houses and bungalows were added in later years, surrounding a central green. We were away from the centre of the village, but it felt like a million miles away from those who lived in the posh private houses.

I have no idea how we managed. There were times when mum was able to get a part-time job, but poor health and looking after three kids prevented her doing anything much. She once worked in our junior school kitchen and later as a cleaner at Bedales School. We never seemed to have any money and she sometimes pleaded for her wages early, which must have been humiliating for her. Often we would walk miles to visit her solicitor to find out if Dad had sent any money. I don't know if he ever did, but I would sit outside the office listening to her pleading and crying. She always cried again on the way home.

What I remember clearly is that we always seemed to be hungry. Often I would steal apples from next door's garden and some nights when my hunger became too much, I would sneak down the stairs and creep into the kitchen to steal a bit of bread and put some sugar on it, hoping it wouldn't be noticed the next morning.

I had to wear my clothes until they fell to pieces. I had holes in my shoes and Mum told me to put newspaper in the soles to stop my feet getting wet. It was like a secret between my mum and me, but in the rain the paper was no protection and it quickly became a soggy mass and fell to bits. I always felt so ashamed about this, fearing that some of the other kids would see the state of my shoes. Already I was the oldest child locally to be wearing short trousers; they were cheaper and we always had to get our money's worth from our clothes. We also had to put whatever we could find on the fire because we couldn't afford coal, and our house was so cold in winter that the insides of the windows would freeze. I used to entertain myself by drawing patterns in the ice with my fingers, melting it with my breath and watching it freeze again instantly.

However, what was worse than the lack of money and food was the lack of love. Mum was a thin, unsmiling, angry woman with a violent temper, whose frustration and resentment at her situation would explode all over us like vomit; cruel, hate-filled words often aimed at my absent dad, but always in my direction. My sisters suffered too but I got the most beatings – at least that was some attention from her. Apparently I looked like him and she hated him. She often screamed at me, 'You're no good; you're just like your dad!' So what was she saying about me?

If you are loved, then perhaps even as a child, you can handle most things together as a family, trying to make the best of the situation. But for us as children, it felt like everything in us was being drained away. All we wanted was love, care, encouragement, positive attention and gratitude for our often futile attempts to please her, but instead we got her vicious tongue and attacks, day after day, year after year, poisoning both soul and mind.

Mum would hit out with anything she had in her hand at the time. Once I got smacked across the head with a thick-bottomed metal pan. My sister still has it, with the dent in the bottom from my head. I'm amazed that I wasn't knocked unconscious. Another time I was spitting angry with Mum for some reason and ran through the kitchen while she was sweeping.

'You silly, old cow,' I yelled, and tried to open the back door to escape. It stuck. I looked round at her and as I did she smashed the broom down on the arm that I had raised to defend myself. It hurt so much that I knew even then it was fractured. But this was sixty years ago when there was no social services support, few routine hospital visits and very little, if any, medication. I was expected to strap it up and cope with the pain. It was my problem, as were any other injuries. I remember one day I was sawing a knotty piece of wood. Suddenly the saw hit a knot in the log, shot up in the air and came down across my left hand which was holding the wood. I ran indoors, blood leaking all over the place, and showed the wound to my mum.

'Well, clean it then, put something on it. I can't stand the sight of blood!' So I washed it and wrapped a handkerchief around it, hoping to stop the bleeding.

Another time I was running around on the front green and tripped over a hump. As I hit the ground my knee smacked into a sharp piece of flint that was sticking up, immediately opening it up like a pair of lips. Looking down I saw the bone of my knee where the flesh had peeled back. I freaked out and ran home, crying and trying to hold the flesh together. But yet again I got no sympathy or help from Mum.

Many years later I went through therapy as part of counselling training for prison work and I was asked: 'What did you have to do to get your mum to say she loved you, or to get any kind of positive affirmation?' I had no idea and, confused by the question, I phoned one of my sisters, who responded without having to think: 'She never ever said that she loved any of us.'

There was only one time I ever remember Mum sticking up for me. We used to have a rag-and-bone man come down our road with his horse and cart, calling out: 'Any old rags.' I was always lippy and would love to run behind him, taking the mick by shouting back 'Any old rags', and laughing at him. He didn't appreciate my humour and one day he caught hold of me and hit me round the head with a stunningly hard blow. I lost it and for a brief moment I flipped, grabbed my penknife from my pocket and stabbed him in the leg.

I have always had a fascination with knives, even to this day. This would later lead to a lot of trouble, but this one, probably my first knife, was a very cheap, children's plastic-coated little thing that didn't do much damage. However, it scratched him enough to draw blood.

He dragged me to our house, threatening me, and banged away on the door in anger. When my mum came he told her that I had stabbed him and showed her the small cut I had made. I was feeling sorry for myself and was crying. I told her that he had hit me hard around the head and she sent him away with a flea in his ear. I have no idea why she stuck up for me on this occasion.

Despite her attitude towards us, I was desperate to please my mum. I tried to do all I could to help out, not because I was good, but because I was longing for a positive stroke. I walked miles to find wild strawberries and violets for her because I knew how much she liked them. In early spring the high banks along one edge of a private field behind our estate would be covered in bluebells and daffodils, and I often stretched my hand through the barbed wire to try and reach some for her. But it seemed that the better flowers were higher up the steep bank, so I carefully squeezed through the wire, trying not to tear my clothes. Further up there was a large white house set back in its own grounds. In my mind I would imagine that this was a commando raid and if gentry started knocking at our house I would be in real trouble! Anyone watching from the house would have spotted a young curly head pop up and then, mysteriously, flower after flower would disappear. I never got caught and I suspect that the posh lady who lived there knew what was going on, although she never said anything. But there was never any gratitude or thanks from Mum, just a dismissive: 'Well, find a jar to put them in then.'

She never seemed to stop complaining about how hard life was for her and the effect on me was like a constant guilt trip. I felt it was my duty to make sure that my two younger sisters were OK and to try and look after Mum. I was the 'man of the house' and, even before I was eight years old, I felt it was expected of me to do a lot of the traditionally male physical jobs.

We had a smallish front garden and a larger one at the back and I felt it was my job to look after them both. I struggled to cut the hedges with shears that were as 'blunt as old Harry'. It was a bit like asking a young child to cut your hair, and the hedge probably looked worse when I finished than before I started. I'd tried and failed and would end up being shouted at for it.

In much the same way I would have a go at cutting the grass. We had a very cheap manual lawnmower and I would lean it into my stomach to get more power behind me. Often the mower would stop – maybe the grass was wet or the mower too blunt – and I would end up with the mower pushing painfully back into my guts. Even now, all these years later, mowing my own lawn brings back some of these negative memories and emotions.

I never knew the difference between weeds and flowers and

I knew nothing about clay soil, which was in our back garden. I would try to attack it with a spade and it would take all the strength I had to get up one small, thick lump that I could barely break down. In a very short time I would be exhausted, drained and would soon give up. The garden could have looked lovely; it sloped down to the bottom where there were trees and a small stream or ditch, but instead, to our mum's shame, we had the best weeds and brambles for miles around. I used to hear the neighbours next door, our mum's friends, moaning about our weeds growing over into their garden. I was really ashamed about this. I felt that I should have been able to do it and I couldn't. And as the brambles grew, so it seemed did the anger and aggression in our mum.

Often when I played in the woods I would bring home the heaviest log I could find to chop up for our Rayburn, thinking it would please her, but it never did. In fact 'wooding' – collecting fallen branches for firewood – was one of my regular jobs. I would push a large, old-fashioned pram to the top of our road and up into the hills and fill it with as much wood as I could find. I didn't enjoy it, but I tried to make it fun wherever I could. If the wood was dry enough and not too thick, I could break it up by stamping on it or by putting it between two trees close together and pushing it round with all my weight until it snapped.

Occasionally other children and their dads would come along and it would be a bit like an expedition. For them it may have been fun, for me it was important: I had to collect as much wood as I could, keeping my eye on the adults, never trusting any of them. The steep banks were hard to come down and I found the best way was to try to hang on to the nearest trees as I worked my way down. Sometimes I had to slide down holding onto tree roots, though this usually meant that my short trousers often got ripped and covered with chalk. That earned me another hiding when I got home.

I used to leave the pram on the road at the bottom of these steep slopes and would gradually manage to fill it completely. The problem then was trying to get down the main road with the heavy load. I had to cling onto the pram to stop it running away. If I let go and it got damaged or hit by a car, I would be in big trouble. I would return home, sweat pouring down my face which was plastered with a grin and an expression which said: 'Look what I've brought home'. I knew how hard it had been and I was proud of my achievements.

'Well, get it cut up then,' was my mum's response to all my efforts. So that would be more hard work sawing logs with the old, blunt bow saw. But even then it seemed like my efforts were in vain. My mum, who was always cold, would load the Rayburn with logs and sit right in front of it with the door open, heat blasting out, while we sat at the back of the room freezing cold. All she would have to do was close the door and the heat would radiate through the top of the solid steel cooker and warm the whole room, providing heat for us all. But it didn't happen. We didn't seem to matter.

Sometimes I would collect stray coal that had fallen from the delivery vans, but Mum also pressurised me into stealing coal from our next-door neighbour. She wouldn't call it stealing – she would start complaining about being cold and tell me to 'go and get some coal from next door'.

The neighbours, he was Scottish, had little to do with us and I never had any trouble from them. But, because I wanted to please Mum, I would creep out in the dark, clamber over the back fence and up to the coal hole by his back door. I would take bits here and there so that he didn't miss any (as if he had memorised every lump) and take back just enough to please Mum. I knew that if the missing coal was noticed, I would be blamed and get a good hiding. What I found confusing though, was that when I grabbed apples from their fruit trees or 'fallers' on the ground to eat because I was so hungry, my mum gave me a beating when she found out. Why was it OK to steal for her to be warm but not for me because I was hungry?

When I was about eight, my mum asked me to take the pram to Petersfield, the nearest town a few miles away to buy some coal. We couldn't usually afford it, but she must have had some extra money. I didn't understand why we couldn't have it delivered, but I felt really pleased, like a 'dog with two tails' being asked to do something so important, that a grown man would normally do.

She explained several times what I had to do. I was to go to the coal yard, pay the money in at the office and ask for half a hundredweight of coal, which is 56lb (25kg). They would give me a chit of paper, which I had to take over to a man by a coal chute and he would pour out the coal into our pram.

The road to Petersfield from Steep is a winding road with almost no pavements and a couple of big hills to tackle on the way back. I didn't take my sisters because the road had fast traffic on it. I didn't give a lot of thought as to how I would manage this. I just knew I had to, somehow.

I arrived at the coal yard and did everything I was asked to do. When I went to the chute to collect the coal, I remember the man who filled the sack for me, his face smudged with coal dust, looking at me in a curious way.

'Who are you with, son?' he said, looking around for an adult.

'No one,' I told him. 'I'm on my own.'

'Got far to go then?'

'Steep.'

I watched his jaw 'bounce' on the ground three times. 'Steep,' he repeated. He was amazed at how far I was expected to take this heavy load. But it felt good that I was being asked to do something hard, impossible even, and I was determined that I would do it. Mum had told me to, so it must be possible.

Leaving the yard was easy at first. The road starts quite flat and then slopes downhill, to where there is now a small roundabout. But then things started to get tough. I clearly hadn't worked out how to get home with such a heavy load. First, a slight incline, but then I came to a very steep hill and had to hold onto garden walls, pushing with all my strength. The pram seemed to weigh a ton and I was so little. I was close to collapsing and felt that I couldn't go any further. I pulled the pram handles to the right and let the wheels come back into the wall, using them to stop me rolling back down the hill. My heart was banging away and the sweat was pouring off me and into my eyes.

'It's too hard. I can't do it,' I kept saying to myself. But I had to. Step by step I struggled up the hill, getting a little bit further and then briefly resting every few steps to gather my strength. I had a long way to go, but every step up was a step nearer to home.

There were no more pavements after that hill, but I was terrified that I would be crushed by a car. I had another road to cross and then back down another hill. What now? Do I run with it and hope that I don't lose the lot, or should I go carefully? I don't know how I managed, but I eventually got home, covered in sweat. Would I get a hero's welcome? Would there be any flags out to greet me? No. There was no pat on the back, no 'Well done', just a look of surprise. It was a wonder the pram survived, let alone me.

One of the few times that I seemed able to please my mum was when she would ask me to join her on the walk to her solicitor in Petersfield. Sometimes when walking with her, she would push me into the gutter if someone was coming the other way. But most of the time I would be skipping and running around her, excited to be spending time with her. Mum's solicitor was down a short alley off the market square and during these visits I was always left outside, trying not to look into the faces of people walking past. For some strange reason I felt guilty being there, this little lost boy in his short trousers, grubby and torn. Inside the office I could hear a man's patient tones and my mother crying in despair. Standing outside I would find it hard not to cry at the sound of my mum in tears, pleading with the man. I know she was desperate for rent money because we were being threatened with eviction.

I never knew the outcome of these meetings, but I know that the journey home was very different from the walk into town. I would be tired out and feeling grumpy. We had walked miles and it had all been a waste of time. Looking at our mum from the corner of my eyes, I would often see her crying. And then the violent explosion happened and she screamed at me: 'See, I told you what your old man is! See what he's like! He doesn't care a fig about you. Do you know that? Do you?'

I wanted to shout out, 'Whoa, hold up! It's not me, it's our dad that you're angry with!'

I hated my home life, but outside the house, things weren't any better. Living in such a middle-class area, we felt like we were the local blight. Posh people don't speak to lesser people like us and we were ostracised, like lepers in a colony. Often these people would ride their horses to the local blacksmith and I would be sat in the gutter writing down car number plates, looking up at these great horses towering above me. I always remember one particular posh woman riding down the road on her horse, looking down her nose at us miserable semi-feral, uninhibited, council-estate kids.

I felt dirty and ashamed of my poverty and really envied the children I saw going to the nearby private schools. They had it made – the clothes on their backs were worth more than we possessed as a family altogether. Once a week we would watch the older teenagers as they went for their cross-country runs past us snotty-nosed kids. Most of the time we were totally ignored and I often wanted to shout at them. I resented their wealth so much. They had everything and we had nothing.

Like many small villages, the general hobby of the inhabitants of Steep was to know everyone else's business. In fact, if you find my old street now on Google Maps, you will see a neighbour staring directly at the camera on several shots. This was a place where curtains would move when I walked down the street. It always felt like they were waiting to have a go at us. Sometimes I would climb one of the oak trees on the green outside our house and suddenly a neighbour – one man in particular just a few doors up from us – would run out, shouting at me and smacking me round the head. Why would an adult sit watching through his net curtain, waiting for the opportunity to come barrelling out of his house, shouting his mouth off at me, just a young child? Did he hate us that much? Even if we sat on the edge of the pavement outside his house he would soon rush out shouting at us, 'Oi you, Greenaway, bog off down to your own end!'

Sometimes I would run along the narrow public footpath between some of the bungalows and a neighbour would burst out of their home shouting, 'Go the other way round,' as if it was a private area.

Two of my dad's sisters had houses just doors away, but wanted nothing to do with us. I remember going to one of their houses a couple of times, but it always felt like we weren't wanted. It wasn't just my dad that rejected us – it was his whole family.

I would often be threatened with the neighbour telling my mum, whether I was guilty of something or not, which always meant a good hiding. I once remember getting beaten for breaking a window I knew nothing about. Mum was never able to listen to my side of the story and she certainly never believed what I said. Later, when she found out that I had told her the truth and that the other person, even an adult, had been lying, I would be told that the hiding I had had would do for next time. It never did of course.

At that time it felt that if anything happened, I was always the one to be blamed, especially with the stigma of not having a dad around. The kids up the road could blame me for what they had done wrong and in the end I decided that if I was going to get blamed and beaten, I may as well do it, whatever 'it' was.

Our junior school was half a mile away, opposite the local church. It was a nightmare and I was bullied like blazes, which continued when I transferred to secondary school. I think my body language – walking with my head down and shoulders hunched – marked me out as an easy target. It felt that every day, either on the way to school or on the way home, I would be picked on or beaten up. One particular kid found out that he could bully me and I wouldn't retaliate – all the fight had been knocked out of me by then – so I became his pet hobby. At the end of the school day on my slow, dreamy walk home, he and a group of kids would be waiting to have a go at me. Many years later when I was in my biker gang I saw this kid again in Petersfield. He caught my eye, went white and quickly disappeared. I could have got my own back and kicked his head in, but instead I just found it amusing.

There were some occasions where things appeared 'normal'. Once a year, the flower show took place, with various events held on Steep common. I sometimes entered the miniature garden competition, making a display on a dinner plate or small tray and occasionally I won something. It was run by decent, friendly people and it felt good to be part of something. But it was over all too soon.

Sometimes I would have a few games with other kids on the green, like hide-and-seek and rounders, which I enjoyed. But I didn't have any confidence to be good at anything and when teams were picked, I hoped and prayed that I wouldn't be one of the last chosen, just to feel that I wasn't totally useless and that I was wanted. But it never happened.

The surrounding countryside was my main means of escape

from everything. I spent hours wandering around there, happy with my own company, no one knowing or caring where I was. I even had my own secret den – a cliff near the woods with a large tree on its edge. Its overgrown roots hanging over the cliff edge hid a deep recess that I could climb into. It felt safe, in this womb-like hiding place. I could listen to people talking as they walked up a nearby path, with no idea at all that I was there.

At home, my failed efforts in the back garden offered me another place to hide. I could bury myself in the stinging nettles and brambles and crawl around in the tunnels I had made. It was another place where Mum couldn't find me.

So often, children that are abused and bullied are afraid to tell anyone, but back in those dark old days, abuse of any kind was never talked about at all. Despite the nosiness of our village, it seemed that nobody really knew what I was going through.

I learnt at a very early age not to trust anyone and to keep away from adults, or I would get hurt. So who could I have trusted with my emotional pain? They didn't understand. They didn't care, so why bother talking about it? I was hurting and I had no skills to deal with it. I was just a kid. It often felt like I had been thrown into a pit and there was no escape. I was powerless to change anything. I believed that I was a good-for-nothing, an unwanted kid who was always in the way, that no one cared about. I believed that there was a God, but that I was so bad that He wanted nothing to do with me and I was going to hell – the ultimate rejection. These were the things reinforced repeatedly by the adults around me: from my real father and his family, from my mother and from the neighbours. All I learned from them was bitterness, anger, rejection and frustration. I couldn't fight it. I just collapsed under its weight.

If you tell someone they are a pig long enough, they will start grunting! When you are told time after time, day after day that you are no good and that you are no better than something unpleasant that someone has just stepped in, you start to believe it and play the part that others are forcing on you. I expected nothing because that was all I was going to get. Only bad things would ever happen to me.

I was a cheeky, gobby kid, which might have been my way of trying to fight back. I wasn't willing to listen to anyone outside the family and would often shout my mouth off. Perhaps it was part of why I didn't get on with anyone. In later years I really didn't care if I offended people. I didn't need friends and couldn't trust anyone, so to get a belt around the head was nothing more than I expected or felt I deserved.

I wasn't much of a thinking kid; I just got on with my life in the confines of a dysfunctional home. But as I grew older, I became desperate for answers. Why did my dad leave? I had no memory of him living with us, so what was married life like for him and Mum? Were they madly in love once? Did they fight a lot? Did Mum's temper drive him away? Was it something that I did wrong? My mum seemed to think that everything was my fault, that I never did anything right, so maybe it all went wrong because of me. And why did his whole family reject us, implying in my mind that he had done the right thing by washing his hands of us? I heard rumours later on that Dad had remarried, had had some more kids and had set up home down near Portsmouth. I eventually found out that he was considered to be a wonderful family man. Why them and not us? Mum didn't tell us anything and so many questions were left unanswered.

Eventually I felt like I was starting to go mad. As the poison levels grew and the insanity started to swamp me, I felt like it was all simmering away inside me and growing into a dangerous monster, screaming to be let out. I was just a runt and not strong enough yet to fight back. But one day, I knew it would be my turn. My time would come.

CHAPTER 2

I'm leaving

Mum's constant ill-health continued, but one day she decided to join a number of us when we went wooding, something she rarely did. We were coming down the last hill, reaching a sharp bend and almost home, when I heard her cry out. She dropped the log that she had been carrying on her shoulder, and I saw that her neck was covered in pus. I had the impression that she had an abscess there which had burst when the log rubbed against her neck. She was taken to hospital and I, along with my two little sisters, were partially cared for by a neighbour, who fed us and put us to bed. We were left on our own every night for a few weeks.

We thought Mum was going to die and we didn't know what was wrong. We visited her in Petersfield Hospital and were told that she had tuberculosis and had to be kept in a cold ward. We found her in an almost empty ward with all the windows open, letting in the freezing air. Knowing how cold she always was, I knew she must have hated it.

In a nearby bed was a friendly old lady with a stomach problem – her stomach was so large I thought that she was pregnant. I didn't understand that old ladies couldn't get pregnant. At least she seemed pleased to see us. But on one visit she had gone and we were told that she had died. This scared us. Did everyone who went into hospital die? Was our mum going to die? With her, life was grim, but without her – how would we cope?

Eventually she came home, to our relief. I later found out

that one of the neighbours who had looked after us had been abusing one of my sisters, but my mum refused to believe it. It was yet another adult we couldn't trust and something else we couldn't talk to Mum about.

Not every adult in my world was untrustworthy, though. There was one particular man I respected and that was our local blacksmith, Mr Moss. He worked about a hundred yards from our home and I passed him every day after school, sometimes saying hello. I loved to visit his forge, look at the bellows and horseshoes on the wall, smell the burning coke and watch him heat up metal in the roaring fire. He made sure I knew my boundaries and I would have to stand back if there was a horse in, but there was never any aggression and I wasn't told to clear off. He was a really good man who gave me positive regard and treated me as an ordinary kid.

Another Good Samaritan was the person who left boxes of food on our front doorstep occasionally at Christmas time. I was convinced that it was the posh lady from whose garden I stole flowers. I thought she was really special. I don't remember any excitement or rejoicing from my mum over this free gift, though. Someone else who was kind to us was Mrs Gough, a farmer's wife who lived nearby. At times my two sisters and I would trudge over the fields to the farm and wait for her to spot us. She would usually be in the kitchen cooking, with the top half of her stable door open. She would call out to us and ask us if we would like some bread and dripping. With our mouths watering, we would watch her cut each of us a wedge of homemade bread and pour on thick dripping out of a tray where she had cooked some meat. I can't begin to say how good that tasted, nor what a precious lady she was. We didn't go too often as we didn't want her to get fed up with us. Many years later I tried to find her to say thank you, but the family had moved on.

Despite most of my dad's family wanting little to do with us, there was one person from that side who treated me differently. Ken Hall was married to one of my dad's sisters and lived nearby. He was a famous scrambler in the region and had won lots of trophies – one was even named after him (The Ken Hall Trophy). He always used to let me sit on his bike and allowed me to ride it when I was about twelve. I once tried to turn it round, bounced up on the green and ended up stalling it. But there was no anger or belittling from him over this. I thought he was really cool and I noticed that people in my neighbourhood treated me differently when he was around and I was on his bike. From that moment, bikes became very special to me.

My mum's side of the family were good to us. Her three brothers were all very different, but treated us well. My mum always talked positively about the one who still lived in Freshwater on the Isle of Wight. He was never warm and gushy, but it felt good to see him and be around him. To me he was a hero and someone to look up to.

Living on the Isle of Wight, my mum's family weren't able to support us much, but I used to spend some of my summer holidays on the Island with my grandparents in Freshwater. Gran always seemed to be busy running a small guest house and spent much of her time in the kitchen. I thought a lot of her, although now I feel that I never really knew her. Our granddad seemed to be a bit of a legend – an ex-poacher and ladies' man. He would be the one keeping an eye on me when I stayed with them, leaving my sisters at home in Steep with Mum.

When my great-gran was alive, I remember watching her making rag rugs, pulling cut-up pieces of old clothing through large sections of sacking, made of hessian. She wasn't able to do much, but to me she was a special person, always willing to have a chat. She somehow disappeared in my memory, and I can't recall being told that she had passed on nor that any funeral had taken place.

My time with my grandparents was always peaceful and happy. The bedroom I slept in was said to be haunted. I thought I heard someone coming upstairs one night and my grandparents said it wasn't them. But the thought of a ghost didn't scare me. It was the living I needed to fear, not the dead. However, even though I didn't like the dark, Gran's house was different. I would sit on the windowsill in my bedroom at night, feet hanging out into space, looking at the stars. It always seemed to be so still and quiet.

But back at home, life was about to change. One day, when I was about eight, I burst into our house through the back door (we never used the front door) and ran through the kitchen into our living room, to see a man I'd never met before sat on the couch looking really uncomfortable. I was surprised – we never had visitors. Mum introduced him. 'This is your new dad. I am marrying him to control you,' she said. Nice introduction, Mum – you must have worked hard at that!

All I could say was the first thought that shot into my mind: 'Ugly, isn't he?'

I wasn't lying. Ronald Shepherd was a very tall, wiry, thin, unpleasant-looking man. But once again, my mind was full of questions. Where did she meet him? When did they go out together? We never saw her 'going out', as it were. We knew that at one time she was in a relationship with one of the local farm workers because I followed her one day and spotted them together. But I knew nothing about this one.

Very quickly he took over the 'man's' jobs in the house that I used to do, which I resented. He then totally decimated our back garden – my refuge and my hiding place. He blitzed everything, taking it down to ground zero. I had nowhere to hide any more.

It was not the best start to a relationship with my so-called 'new dad'. For a short while I was encouraged to follow him around, going into Petersfield at times, perhaps even going wooding with him. But it didn't take long before he started to beat me under my mother's instructions, usually with the thick leather belt he wore all the time.

And pretty soon their own relationship deteriorated too. The only time I really heard Mum laughing was when two council workmen threatened to knock my old man's teeth out. I couldn't understand why that was funny. The joke was, apparently, that he could take them out himself – he had false teeth. But it confused me that someone threatened him with violence and she just laughed. I don't remember any affection between them and I would often hear her shout at him. I have no idea why he would want to come into this situation. Who would want to marry a woman like that who already had three kids?

When I was about twelve, I managed to get some work clearing a lady's overgrown back garden. She asked me to remove the weeds and nettles, but I cut her lawn too, which she wasn't happy about. She had only wanted the nettles removing. I'd got it wrong again. Sometime later I knocked on her door again to see if there was something else I could earn money for. There was no answer, so I looked round the back of the house. She wasn't there. I spotted an open window, climbed through and stole a few little things. It seemed so simple and I was good at it. It was an easy way of getting money – or so I thought.

I was already known to the police by then because of petty crime, such as breaking windows and petty theft. It all started when I began 'borrowing' someone's bike. A guy from up in the hills behind us would ride down to Steep, hide his bike and catch the bus into Petersfield. I got to know where he left it and I took it for a ride round the village and put it back before he returned; we never had our own bikes. But one day a local cop caught me, questioned me, slapped me around a bit and took me home where I got slapped again. I don't think I got nicked for that, but the bike owner never left his bike there again.

Sometime later two heavy cops appeared at our door. I ended up with 'my collar being felt' as they questioned me about the burglary at the lady's house that I had worked at. In the end I put my hands up, told them I had done it and that I was sorry. The truth was that I was sorry I'd got caught.

I appeared in Petersfield Magistrates' Court (now a museum) and was put on probation. I was especially lucky that I was given a very good probation officer. Nowadays, it seems to me a probation officer is only able to enforce the law, and many lads end up back in prison because of something they have told their probation officer – but back then it was more of a supportive role. I had to report to him once a week to let him know how I was getting on and at times he would visit me at home to see how things were. Suddenly, and perhaps for the first time, I had someone who was interested in me. He really seemed to listen to me and I even felt that I could trust him and tell him how I was feeling, what I wanted for my future and my dreams of escaping and joining the navy. That was a new experience. I began to look forward to reporting in to him. I guess if anything, it felt like I had a proper father figure in my life. If only my real father had been able to watch and learn.

One day I came home and he was there on an unexpected visit, chatting to my mum.

'You know we have talked about your wanting to join the navy when you leave school?' he said.

I nodded in surprise. I was still only thirteen.

'I wondered what you thought about a boarding school in Southampton, not too far from the docks. It would give you a good idea of what it would be like to live away from home and whenever you wanted, you could go down to the docks and see the boats.'

I told him that sounded good. So a few days later, I found

myself bundled in his car to go to a Dr Barnardo's home for boys in Shirley, Southampton. It felt special that he cared enough to take me to this place himself. It felt like a long journey and finally we arrived at a big, posh, white house, surrounded by a high wall. We drove up the drive, past well-kept lawns and fir trees. I felt very nervous. I believed that it was a home for orphans, so I felt a bit strange knowing that I wasn't one. It turned out to be a boys' home for around ten boys who had at least one parent. Running it was the master, with his wife and two daughters. The home seemed to be a good place – at least there was no more violence or shouting – *or so I thought.*

The school I would be going to was within walking distance and at first everything was OK, until another bully there started picking on me, sensing I wouldn't fight back.

And the home wasn't violence-free either. I remember looking out of the window in shock, watching the master chasing one of the older, bigger guys around the front garden. It suddenly felt like being back at home, seeing the insanity of violence and aggression again.

Apart from that I felt proud to be living in such a nice place after my impoverished family home. I thought maybe people on the outside would think I was posh and treat me differently. I was better dressed than I had ever been before and was being taught good manners. We were allowed to go out on our own at weekends. I made friends with some orphan twins a few years older, who taught me how to play the fife. I felt for the first time in my life I could do something. I was given permission to practise in the drying room at the back of the house, which was a large airing room filled with damp washing. I wouldn't disturb anyone there and again I was on my own, so I felt safe.

I joined the Boys' Brigade band and I can remember with pride marching in a parade through the streets of Southampton. We were also part of activities at the local Baptist church.

Considering how my life turned out, it was surprising that the spiritual message of the church left me completely untouched. I had previously recited prayers by rote at junior school, but none of it reached me. I believe these situations were opportunities missed by adults to share the real gospel with us.

In those days, our milk was still delivered by horse-drawn cart, which was becoming quite old-fashioned even back then. I used to love visiting the local dairy, which had a lot of horses. The dairy staff treated me really well and let me spend time in the stables stroking the horses. They also had a very bright room where several ladies would be checking eggs. When they saw my curiosity, they explained that they were looking for bad eggs, which could be spotted under strong light and thrown away. What really sticks in my mind was being treated as a normal polite kid and not being told to clear off with a clip around the ears.

For the other kids the weekends meant something else which I didn't realise at first. I came back one Saturday to see the master standing at the back door with a billiard cue in his hands, looking furious. He was clearly waiting for someone. I found out that a group of the lads would often go out shoplifting on Saturdays and they had become well known in the area. Now the master was waiting for them and they were in deep trouble. It scared me in some ways. I'd had enough of violence and I didn't have any interest in shoplifting. Why? I had all that I needed. And I didn't need much. At that time of my life, all I wanted was to feel safe and to be left alone.

From the window of my bedroom that I shared with three other boys I could see the yard of a large haulage firm and I enjoyed watching the lorries sheeting up in the early hours of the morning when the drivers ran large tarpaulin covers over their loads. In my fantasy all I wanted was to have enough bottle to hide away on the back of a lorry, to get under those tarpaulin sheets and to escape this crazy world.

Another thing I enjoyed, which was what drew me to Southampton in the first place, was going down to the dry docks and at times seeing some great boats. I would dream about getting away on one of these, but in reality it showed me that sea life wasn't for me. Being trapped on board with all those people and no escape would have driven me nuts.

One Saturday afternoon I was practising my fife in the drying room when I heard familiar voices. It was my mum and stepdad talking to the lady of the house. I felt very embarrassed. They had managed a rare visit, even bringing a few sweets. My mum asked me several times if I was all right and if I liked it there. Of course I said I was happy, but it felt very strange to have this brief visit. I didn't want it. It seemed to me that they were trying to show they were good parents and that all the problems had been down to me. But I felt like it was them who had rejected me and sent me away.

Eventually, after a couple of years at the home, I was 'demobbed' at the age of fifteen. I was given a new suit and I attended the Dr Barnardo's headquarters in London for a farewell service.

Back at home it felt really odd to see my two sisters again, who now seemed like strangers to me, and when I spoke for the first time to my stepdad, I called him 'sir'. I am grateful to Dr Barnardo's for teaching me some decent manners and confidence, and even the neighbours told me I walked differently – head up, shoulders back, no longer slouching or afraid.

But I found myself once again spending time alone in the woods, wandering through the many places that I knew well as a child. My probation officer seemed intent on getting me off to a good start and got me a job working on a building site constructing a reservoir on the other side of the hills to where I lived. The boss seemed to be surprised that the probation officer was there as my spokesperson, but he offered me the job of tea boy. It didn't take me long to do my chores and I felt chuffed to bits as I wandered around the site, realising that downhill from there was where I used to go wooding as a small child. It would only take me a short time to run home at the end of the day.

I loved to watch the steel erectors working as they tied iron bars together with wire. These would then be taken down the site by a dumper truck and fixed to other iron fittings already slotted into place, in order to build up the reservoir walls. I enjoyed seeing it all taking shape. I also watched an old man building wooden shutters needed to contain the concrete poured around the steel reinforcing frames – I had known his son from years ago from our small estate. He was very skilled and I would watch, fascinated, as he screwed wooden shutters together, clearly taking pride in his work.

I tried to do more than just making the tea and cleaning the hut. Whenever shuttering needed slotting into place, it had to be treated with some oil – a releasing agent – so that once the concrete had hardened, the wooden shutters could be removed. I would try to do this job and it seemed to me to be like a work of art as it all fitted together.

Close to the tea hut was a giant cement mixer and in front of that were huge piles of aggregate, sand and bags of cement. Fixed to the cement mixer was a big electric shovel and I enjoyed trying to work this when I could. I was still just a pimply fifteen-year-old, but when I was allowed, I would pull out the shovel which was on a strong wire, pull the shovel to the side of the heap of sand or shingle, push it into the sand and press the button to wind it in. It wasn't easy. It seemed the shovel had a mind of its own, and I had to pull back as it got nearer to the mixer, so that it would lift up. That was tough for a young kid, but I loved it.

I got on well with most of the guys and I would always try to help where I could and learn more. Eventually I got the job of working the mixer, as well as making tea, which was a lot more hectic. It was a great job and I was paid good money. In fact, I took my mum to the pictures with my first pay packet. But it also meant I didn't have to stay at home all the time, although going to the pictures on my own in Petersfield wasn't easy. It was a mile-and-a-half walk with no streetlights, so at night I walked in the middle of the road, whistling to pretend that I wasn't really as scared as I felt.

However, it wasn't long before things started to fall apart. Six months into the job, I came home one evening to find my stepdad about to smash a milk bottle over my mum's head. My youngest sister was behind him, hanging onto what little hair he had left on my and pull him away from her. I rushed in front of Mum to try and stop him, and he punched me in the face, splattering blood all over me.

'Right, that's it. I'm going to call the police!' I yelled, running out of the house towards a nearby phone box.

'Please don't call them,' my old man pleaded, running after me. But it didn't stop me.

Back at home, Mum shouted, 'What did you call them for? We don't want the police around here.' Her son was standing there, with blood streaming down the front of his shirt from a broken nose, and she was more worried about what people thought of her than me! As soon as she saw the police car, she snarled: 'You called them, you get rid of them.'

Deeply ashamed I went out and explained to the two young officers that my mum had told me to tell them to go away, that they weren't needed. They looked at me covered in blood, with real concern on their faces.

'If this ever happens again, you call us. Don't be afraid to do that,' they told me. I was really touched by the fact that they, the 'enemy', were being so nice to me and cared about me.

I walked into the house fuming. I had tried to stop Mum

getting a good hiding, ended up getting punched myself – and she didn't give a monkey's about me. I had been feeling so much more positive about life after leaving Dr Barnardo's. I'd learned good manners and gained confidence, I had a good job earning my own money and I was respectful to my stepfather, calling him 'sir'. Then suddenly I walked back into this intense anger and violence once again. I couldn't take it anymore.

I didn't even look at my stepdad.

'That's it! I'm leaving. I'll get my money at the end of the week and then I am out of here!' But yet again, my mum was only concerned about herself.

'What about the police? Won't we get into trouble if you leave home so young?' she kept asking. I had to reassure her over and over again that there was no problem in me leaving home.

But in my mind I knew that there was. At the children's home, we'd never been taught any domestic skills. Now I would have to look after myself.

At work I handed in my notice. My boss was a great guy, but I couldn't give him a reason for my leaving. I didn't want him to know my shame. By Friday evening I had packed a change of clothes and a few possessions, and left home for the last time. I was fifteen years old. I had little money and no plans of where to go or what to do. All I knew for sure was that I wasn't wanted, and nobody cared about what happened to me.

CHAPTER 3

Someday, someone will pay

Heading towards Petersfield I took a farm track into some nearby fields. It was getting dark and in the far corner of the field I spotted a hayrick – a stack of cut and baled hay which I thought could make a bed for the night. I struggled to climb to the top and pulled out two bales, leaving a grave-sized shape that I could climb into. It was the middle of winter and freezing cold, but here I would be safe and could sleep. But I couldn't sleep. So many negative thoughts were running round in my head.

I eventually drifted off, but woke up in the middle of the night covered in snow. It was pitch black and I was freezing. I had brought no food with me and I was starving hungry. And worse still, the warmth of my body had attracted swarms of insects and bugs living in the hay – I had been bitten to pieces. Lying there in my 'grave', cold, hungry and miserable, the stark reality of my situation suddenly hit me.

I could die here and no one would know.

I had never felt so alone, so unwanted. No one cared about me. I felt like I was a piece of dirt, mentally subnormal, a leper. The positive impact of the probation officer and the others who were kind to me had vanished. I was worthless, someone to be shunned and ignored. No wonder all those posh, horsey people had looked down on me; no wonder I was bullied, mocked and blamed for everything; no wonder Dad had washed his hands of me and his family had turned their backs on me. And my 'mother'? Now there's a funny word. Isn't a mother someone who is supposed to care for you, look after you, keep you safe and love you? Yeah, right!

All my experiences paraded like ghosts before me and suddenly it felt like there was a 'click' inside my mind – a profound light-bulb moment:

Someday, someone would pay!

And I wouldn't just slap them round the head like the adults in my childhood, or take my belt off and beat them, like my stepfather. No, I would cripple them – scar them so much that every future breath they took would be an agonising, fearful and watchful one. They would all grow older and weaker; I would grow older and stronger. One day I would make them all pay and to hell with the consequences. What more could anyone do to me? I carried enough pain for anyone. Beating me would be no big deal – I'd had it all of my life. If I ended up in prison, would it be worse than my life now?

This was the most memorable day of my life so far. The growing furnace of hate and anger had come to a head, turning me into some kind of animal. I was fired by the seething frustration I had felt for so long of feeling powerless and unable to defend myself. The monster was ready to come out. It would later be given full permission to lash out when the drugs and drink kicked in and my inhibitions disappeared. But for now, the worm had turned. I was ready.

I lived rough for a while, sleeping in the backs of covered lorries that were left in a local car park overnight. I believe some of the drivers found out what I was doing and suddenly thick coats were left in the back on the seats of the vehicles for me to cover myself and keep warm. Their kindness blew me away.

I decided to go to Northampton to visit a girl I had met on

my last holiday on the Isle of Wight. We had promised to keep in touch, so I called her and used what little money I had for the 110-mile train journey. I still had next to nothing, so when I met her I explained what had happened and told her that I needed somewhere to live. She knew of a few places and took me to a place in a back street, run by some foreigners. Jabbering away in their own language, they showed me a small room with a tiny kitchen. I couldn't afford the rent so they showed me a cheaper one, which was little more than a cupboard with a fold-down bed. They promised to supply a heater, which turned out to be an electric hotplate, the size of a small saucepan. At least I could cook food – not that I had anything to cook with.

The owners asked my age. 'Sixteen and a half, nearly seventeen,' I lied. I think they knew I was a runaway.

I had to stay in most of the time, because I couldn't afford to eat out and it was freezing outside. The electricity was metered and I soon discovered that the hotplate devoured electricity. Fortunately I managed to find work in a local car valve factory. I was the youngest worker there and it was noisy and hot, but at least I was earning some money. But after the rent and meter money, I had little left for food and lived off tins of soup and beans.

I can remember walking to work, shuffling my feet along in the snow and ice, head down, not looking at anyone, feeling cold and rejected. I had been better off in the children's home! I was sick in my guts with all the raw emotions that I carried and filled with loathing for everything and everyone. Even a laugh in the street or a smiling face would spark off paranoia and raw anger, reminding me of anyone who had ever laughed at me and mocked me as a child. And why should they be happy when I was so damned miserable?

It didn't take long for my poor diet and unhealthy lifestyle to make me ill. I had chronic diarrhoea, became too weak to work or eat and just lay on my bed feeling like a rung-out dish rag.

39

Then I remembered the gold dress studs. A few months previously I had broken into an empty house and stolen them. One was set with a big pearl and the other had what appeared to be a diamond the size of a pencil end. What if I could sell them? I could afford to eat some decent food then.

Still feeling awful, I struggled into a nearby jeweller's shop and showed him the diamond stud.

'What's your name, son?' he asked. Without thinking I gave him both my name and address.

'And where did you get this?'

I told him that my gran had left it to me in her will.

'Come back in a week. I'll do some tests and tell you what it's worth.'

By the time I left the shop, all my alarm bells were banging away. Rushing home I hastily packed and made my way to the railway station. I remembered one of the guys who I had worked with on the reservoir building site had gone to work in a hotel near East Wittering, Chichester. I decided to try my luck and headed to West Sussex. As soon as I arrived, there it was right in front of me, close to the sea front – the Shore Inn. I found the boss and he offered me a job as a kitchen porter. It was the bottom rung of the ladder, but I would have board, food and even money.

Most of the work was washing up and serving food. After a few weeks, I was offered a job as a still-room porter, working in a small room washing the silver and glassware. It was a hot and sticky environment, but I always enjoyed working and was determined to do a good job.

Near the hotel was a biker cafe, where I spent a lot of my time. I didn't have a bike, but they accepted me and I loved the noise and power of their bikes. I made a few friends, but I also started making enemies. The temper I had both inherited and learned from my mum was rearing its ugly head and I started lashing out with little excuse. I began to be labelled as a bit of a nutter.

After some time I was summoned to the boss' office where two young 'suits' were waiting to question me about the dress stud. I was impressed. I had no idea how the police had tracked me down from Northampton, which was more than a hundred miles from Chichester. I was in deep trouble.

'How much is it worth?' my boss asked quietly.

'About £200,' he was told. That was a lot of money back then.

I crumbled under their questioning and admitted taking the pin. I handed over the pearl one as well, thinking my honesty would make things better. It probably made it worse.

Pretty soon I was back in Petersfield Magistrates' Court again. Surprisingly, my stepfather turned up and started sticking up for me. He'd never done anything like that before. I was convinced that I was going to get probation again. But I was wrong.

'You will do three months in a detention centre, Greenaway,' ordered the magistrate.

My stepfather looked close to tears, but I couldn't see what all the fuss was about. It was going to be just like the children's home, wasn't it? What was there to be worried about? The two young police officers escorting me out were talking to me and trying to be nice, as if they felt sorry for me. What for? I could do this standing on my head!

Arriving at Haslar Detention Centre, in Gosport, Hampshire (now Haslar Immigration Removal Centre), we drove up to metal gates that seemed to reach up into the sky. The huge perimeter fence had rolls of barbed wire across the top. I could feel the tension from the police officers. Hold on, this can't be the right place, I wanted to say. As the gate swung open, I saw a large tarmac area like a parade ground with flower borders round the sides in perfect straight lines. Everything looked so clean and sterile. Once inside, papers were exchanged, the police officers left, wishing me luck, and I was handed my grey prison uniform.

'Right, lad, run a bath, get cleaned up and put your clothes in this box,' said the prison officer in a calm voice. I did what he asked and he sat unconcerned nearby, concentrating on a crossword. This wasn't so bad if they were all as nice as him! It really was like Dr Barnado's.

After my bath, he looked at me. 'OK, ready now, lad?'

I nodded and he took me through a door and back outside.

'See that door over there?' he said, pointing across the parade ground. 'I WANT YOU TO MARCH TO IT. IF YOU DON'T DO IT RIGHT, WE'LL BE HERE ALL NIGHT UNTIL YOU DO!' He yelled so loudly they must have heard him in Portsmouth! What happened to the decent guy I had seen earlier? Suddenly I realised I wasn't in another kids' home; I was in boot camp.

Down endless corridors, through door after door unlocked and locked again, I was finally taken to the reception rooms where I was to spend the next few days. Brick built with large glass windows looking out onto the corridors, they were where new prisoners were monitored for drugs or mental health issues. The next day, when I was let out, I glanced at the guy in the next cell. It looked like he was asleep, but his arm was hanging off the side of his bed. Underneath I saw a large pool of blood dripping from his slashed wrist. I shouted for help and quickly we were all banged up again. Nothing much was said about the incident, but he survived. I got to know him later. He wasn't really suicidal, just a bit of a nutter who would entertain us with antics like making his shorts fall down when we went out running.

On that first morning, I was taken to the barber's room with the other reception prisoners. I hadn't taken too much notice of the others in the detention centre. I was first in the queue.

'How do you want your hair?' I was asked.

'Do you know what a Boston is?' I said. He nodded.

'Short and tidy, OK lad?' I heard the trimming shears warm up and touch the back of my neck. He's going to tidy the back, I thought. But no, he was straight over from the back of the neck to the front in a number one – the shortest of cuts. Suddenly I had the opposite of a Mohican: a landing strip in the centre of my hair. The rest of it soon ended up on the floor. I wanted to attack him. I always liked having my hair long and was funny about anyone touching it. At least the screws (prison officers) in here had a sense of humour!

Life in the detention centre was about breaking us down and building us into someone different, but tough hardly comes close to describing it. The day started early with a freezing cold wash and shave, before marching to the parade ground for exercises before breakfast. We were forced to do bunny hops until our legs burned with pain, all the time being yelled at by the guards, who seemed to hate us.

Every day there was relentless exercise and training. We were forced to run a mile, gasping to the finish line. Our time was noted and we were expected to better it each week. We did circuit training in the gym; weights, push-ups, bunny hops and jumps for five minutes each. At the end of the first few whistles, we began to wish we were dead. And of course, if we succeeded, our time and the repetitions would be increased. At the end of each session we would be shovelled up from the sweaty heap on the ground that we had become.

I was put to work stripping old carburettors in a scrap metal room. We had to separate each different metal component into various dustbins, which I thought had to be the most boring job in the detention centre. And the vicious, bullying screws would constantly swoop down on us and check, snarling at us if we dared to get it wrong.

After a few days I was moved into the main dorm, where

we had to keep our bed spaces in perfect order. The guards examined them in minute detail and anything out of place would be sent flying across the room. I got to know some of the other lads and we had a good laugh. A couple of soldiers were in there, who taught us dirty songs that we all sung when the lights went out.

Very soon I was put in charge of the dorm – they had obviously spotted my leadership qualities! I must be doing something right. Either that or they felt sorry for me. But then the huge screw who had promoted me explained that if there were any problems in the dorm, I was the one who would be blamed and punished. It didn't feel so good any more.

It wasn't long before I found out what this meant. A couple of lads were joking and laughing one night after lights out and suddenly the door was thrown open.

'Greenaway, get out here!' bellowed the screw.

'But it wasn't me,' I spluttered.

I was marched into the corridor in my pyjamas. 'I told you, Greenaway, any bother at all it's down to you,' he bellowed into my face, punching me in the guts. I fell against the corridor wall. I was threatened with being sent to the 'block' where we'd heard rumours of brutal beatings.

'You will stand to attention here until I come back for you,' he yelled and disappeared. I could have leaned on the wall, or even sat down, but I knew how quiet these guys could move and catch you out. Finally, as the cold started to eat into me and my legs were at the point of collapsing, he came back. 'Right, back inside and no more noise, OK?'

Back in the dorm, as soon as the door slammed, I grabbed my hobnailed boots and laid into the lads who had been making a noise. They didn't retaliate or say anything. No one was going to mess things up for me again.

Every Sunday we had a church parade, where we had to stand

to attention as the governor checked us over.

'Nice clean boots, lad,' the governor said to me on my first Sunday. That felt good, he seemed like a nice guy.

'Did you rub them on the back of your trousers?'

I didn't dare lie.

'Yes, sir,' I admitted. I should have cleaned them properly before inspection, rather than just a quick rub on my trousers while standing in line. That got me into trouble, having black marks on my trousers.

I was also pulled up for looking out of the first-floor chapel window. Outside I could see the Solent, the strait between the Isle of Wight and the mainland, where I watched the boats going by and longed to be out there. A tap on the shoulder, a growl from a screw and I was nicked again! I raged inside.

It was horrendously tough, but after a while, I began to enjoy the punishing exercise routine. I was getting a high from the natural chemicals produced and I was building up strong muscles. But we still hated all the screws as much as they seemed to hate us. I thought if I ever met one on the outside, I would really show him. There were two I hated with a passion. One was a small and very slightly-built officer and, with all the originality of prisoners, we nicknamed him 'rat face'. Another was the opposite, about six feet four with a big build. Both these officers I was to meet years later. 'Rat face' became a senior officer in Wandsworth and the other ended up in Exeter, where I was later banged up. I remembered him and went over to speak to him.

'I know you, sir,' I said.

'You don't know me at all, boy,' he snarled.

'Yes I do, sir. Haslar?' He gulped and disappeared.

On the day of my release I felt like I was being demobbed from the army. But when I handed in my uniform and dressed in my own clothes, it felt like they had shrunk. I had only served two months, which had seemed like a lifetime, but I had shot up and bulked out. I walked out past the lads in the exercise yard feeling like a freak, with my trousers barely covering my calves, but I didn't care. I was free.

I had grown in more ways than one. In truth Haslar had blown my mind, and I felt that there was no way that I was going to get in trouble again and end up back in prison. How wrong I was.

Gang Warfare

Leaving the detention centre, I returned to the hotel near East Wittering – the boss had said in court that he would have me back 'on the out'. But after a while I left in protest when a friend was sacked, and I ended up getting a kitchen job in a nearby holiday camp. But there was thieving among the staff and after a sudden police raid, I knew I had to get out. I hadn't done anything wrong, but as an ex-con I couldn't risk being around trouble. I found it soon enough though in my next job, working on a travelling fairground. It was here that I learned more brutal fighting techniques from some of the other lads. They also showed me how to rob customers by short-changing them – if they protested, a smack in the mouth usually settled the argument.

Around this time I used to hang out with a mate who had a bike and sidecar, which was little more than a plank of wood fixed to a frame. But I loved the sense of freedom it gave me when we tore around like a pair of lunatics, hitting every corner hard. Once he struck a kerb when we were trying to get a closer look at a plane coming into land and I flew up into the air, landing with a splat on the pavement.

It was on one of these mad trips that I saw my first Hell's Angels. My mate and I had gone down to the coast where riots were going on between rival gangs – mods and greasers. The Hell's Angels were something different. I'd heard about their reputation before and was a huge fan of Sonny Barger, the president of the Californian Angels. I understood that he took nothing from anyone and was always brutal in dealing with any trouble that came his way. He became my hero – in truth my god. But seeing Hell's Angels up close for the first time and watching how they fought made a lasting impression on me. I wanted to be like them.

However, I was still trying hard to be respectable. I had a steady girlfriend and found a job with the Southern Electricity Board as a labourer. I loved working outdoors, erecting poles and hanging wires, and at the age of twenty-one I was promoted to linesman, the youngest one in the company.

Once I was working on an emergency repair at Seal, near Aldershot, in the middle of a major snowstorm. The lines and poles had blown down and the electricity supply had been cut off. About five gangs were called out to work together repairing it. I suddenly found that at the bottom of my pole was my stepfather, working as one of the labourers, waiting to send equipment up to me on a line. This was an opportunity that I had waited for. Now I could seriously injure him. I threw a hacksaw down that missed his head by inches but then decided to get on with the work. It was a bit of a childish act, and I pulled myself together. The work was more important than our differences.

It was a job I loved because at lunchtimes I could wander away into the countryside. I remember one day sitting very quietly with my back to a tree and watching a deer and her fawn come up to a small pond to drink.

Life was good and I'd even started wearing suits – something I'd never done before. But my temper was getting worse. I remember coming home late one night and a couple of guys laughed at me as I ran for the bus in my best clothes, holding my umbrella. Nobody laughed at me! I jumped on them and punched one very hard in the mouth. His tooth came through his upper lip, but I still had a go at him for the split knuckle his tooth had given me.

Around that time my girlfriend and I moved to what I believe is now Europe's biggest council estate, Leigh Park, a large suburb of Havant, about eight miles northwest of Portsmouth. It was the kind of place where you ended up believing in Superman, because so often you would pass a pub and a guy would come flying through the window!

As usual I gravitated towards bikers, and our numbers grew steadily. When a new youth club, the Point Seven, opened, we used it to set up a bikers' club with about eighty-four guys. But I wanted more than a bike club, I wanted a gang, so I pruned it down to a hard core of guys I could trust and believe in, and we became an unaffiliated Hell's Angels' chapter, based on Sonny Barger's Californian gang. I was voted in as their president and we elected other officers to play important roles in the club.

In order to be part of the gang, you had to at least ride illegally with no insurance or tax, but I worked hard at making us the hardest gang in the area. I started attracting more attention from the police, and was stopped and searched regularly. Once I whispered to the girl on the back of my bike to give a false name and address. It didn't work!

'Hello, Brian, what's going on? What are you up to?' was the response from a copper.

'No, you're mistaken, officer. I'm not Brian Greenaway – I'm Fred Bloggs!'

Most of the fights were with local rival gangs, mainly the mods. In a funny kind of way I respected some of these. They would come looking for us, or we would go down into Havant where they hung out. We would find their scooters and take them for joy rides. I was often surprised that something with such a small engine and little wheels could be such fun, though I would never admit that to anyone at the time!

After a couple of good years, my life started to go downhill rapidly when I began taking drugs. It quickly became a powerful force in my life, giving the monster in me full permission to come out and play. I was sacked from the electricity board for beating up a ganger who was throwing his weight around, and my long-term relationship also ended. Every day became a day of violence: kicking rivals to pieces, hitting them with iron bars, slashing them with knives and attacking them with the chrome-plated German helmet I sometimes wore. It was totally insane. By then I was well known to the police and to other gangs, and every so often guys would try to build up their own reputations by attacking me whenever they could. Once, when I was in the car park of our club, chatting to my mates, I was approached by a couple of rivals. One of them lunged at me with a broken bottle. I whipped off my heavily studded belt – kept free of the loops in my jeans for moments like this – and smashed him around the head. He dropped the bottle and disappeared.

'Now, where was I?' I said, turning back to my mates. They creased up laughing.

Another time, we were told that a local gang member had been done over and was on crutches. Although he was from a rival gang, he was also a Leigh Park biker, part of our joint territory, so we had to retaliate, especially when we found out it had been done by guys pretending to be Hell's Angels.

High on drugs, with a van full of weapons and bikes, we set off on a revenge mission to the pub in Gosport where they hung out. I struggled to breathe from the adrenalin pumping through me as the van tore across roundabouts and veered over busy roads, followed by more of our guys on bikes. We screamed to a halt on the pavement opposite the pub and walked across the road, stopping traffic. They were waiting for us. Instantly a bloody fight broke out, attracting crowds of onlookers watching in horror.

In the middle of all this, some guy from the enemy side was trying to say something to me.

'What?' I asked, pausing.

'I'm only here to keep the peace,' he said.

But as I got ready to pile in again, I saw him out of the corner of my eye swinging a crutch in my direction.

'Keep a piece of this then,' I snarled, grabbing a nearby rounder's bat and smashing it into him. I was enjoying this! He fell to the ground covered in blood, with one of his legs hanging over the pavement. I jumped up and crashed down on it.

Once we'd given them a good thrashing, we shot off back to Leigh Park. This wasn't the last we would hear of this, though. Just a few days later I was in our local cafe, the Friar Tuck, when a couple of 'suits' appeared – clean cut, young and not very confident. Someone said it was the law. I was already smashed out of my head and getting angry.

'Come on guys, let's give them a kicking,' I laughed, getting up. No one moved. I looked around. No one wanted to know; they had had enough of me and my insanity.

I slowly walked past the two officers, asking them who they were looking for. They followed me out to the car park and they told me they were looking for Brian Greenaway. I laughed at them and goaded them, trying to get them to have a go at me so I could wipe them out. None of my mates appeared, although there had been a lot of them in the cafe. I could handle it; who needed them anyway?

After some time they realised that they had the right guy, but they didn't know how to deal with me. Suddenly a marked police car pulled up full of our local cops, and I knew it was time to leave quietly with them. I was coming very close to getting a savage kicking from these guys. I was the only one who had been identified in the fight out of all of our gang – I was arrested and held for questioning.

One evening we had gatecrashed a local school dance and I was at the side of the stage, cutting the power repeatedly so that the band couldn't play. Finally one of them came over.

'We're having some aggro with the electrics, mate. Can you keep an eye on it for me and make sure no one touches it?

'No problem,' I smiled. I was impressed with their psychology. The only way they could possibly stop me was to ask for my help.

Before long a couple of guys swaggered over to me. 'You Greenaway?' they asked, clearly looking for trouble. I wasn't sure if I could take them both.

'He's over the other side of the room,' I told them. They swaggered away and started laughing. That did it! Inside I freaked, shooting from one to ten on the anger scale in a nanosecond. Running towards them, I jumped and drop-kicked them both, knocking them to the ground. They quickly got up, but they had lost interest and didn't want to play anymore. It was all over. We decided to split – the old bill would be around soon.

Outside, car-loads of cops had arrived and as I jumped onto to my bike, a Panther 600cc combo with a side car, a couple of cops came over.

'Your bike, then?' they asked.

'Of course,' I smiled. I was on a high and was willing to go as far as they wanted.

'Were you on it earlier today?' (I had tried to run over a cop who had stood in the road trying to stop me.) I gave a meaningless grunt and for some reason, they backed off and suddenly didn't want to know. I guess that with my mates around me, they didn't want to risk a riot.

But as my insanity increased, I didn't just attack in revenge or to defend myself. I attacked without reason. One Christmas I was wandering around in Havant. Christmas was always a miserable time, even as the president of the Angels. Most of my mates would be with their families and I would be on my own. I wasn't in the best of moods. Coming towards me were a couple of suits off to work in the City like robots, all stamped from the same mould. I had nothing but contempt for them. But then they started laughing. That did it! Bang, I was gone and the red mist hit me. This was the monster at its most dangerous. It wasn't just anger shooting from zero to ten, it was a complete and very frightening insanity where I lost awareness of anything around me. I have been told that my eyes became ice cold and impenetrable. It was so severe that if you had put a gun to my head and shot me through my brain, I felt as though I still could have bitten your hand off. And the suits had caused it by laughing! They had to pay. Without warning I smashed my crash helmet into their faces, leaving them lying in the gutter, covered in blood. A mate across the road saw what happened and ran over.

'What's happening, Brian? What did they do?'

'Oh, nothing. Just didn't like them.'

Another time I was driving past someone in a uniform waiting at a bus stop. I leapt out of the car, ran across the road and chain-whipped him with a bike chain. He was screaming at me to stop. But I couldn't stop. The uniform represented authority and I hated authority.

Of course that hatred included my old enemy, the police. Once at our local pub, the Lord Palmerston in Portsmouth, someone whispered in my ear that the old bill were hanging around outside the toilets. They had already searched some of our guys for drugs. I saw an opportunity to get stuck in – they were dressed in civvies so I steamed in with some of my gang. 'Hey guys, look – poofs hanging around the toilets. Let's do 'em!' I said, lashing out at the one nearest to me. Clearly we had caught them by surprise – it was at the back of the pub where it was very dark.

'Stop, stop! We are police officers,' they shouted at us. I ignored them for as long as I could and eventually they apologised to us. I told them not to do it again and walked off grinning at them.

This was the one and only time that we got away with a bit of GBH on the old bill.

But they always got me in the end. One time when they approached us, a knife fell out of my pocket. They arrested me and my mate, Steve, and his dad came down and bailed us both. I decided to do a runner and ended up in France for six months, hanging round with a group of hippies and having a laugh.

But as soon as I returned home I was arrested and banged up in Winchester Prison – my first adult sentence. This was in a different league to the detention centre, and I'd heard stories of brutal cons, man rape and stabbings.

The prison smelt of sweat and boiled cabbage. Screws stood guard, wearing slashed peak caps pressed against their nose. Some were chewing gum and others wore mirrored sunglasses, trying to look hard. I don't know who they were trying to impress, but it didn't work.

I looked warily around at the crowds of lads. Suddenly I noticed one I knew from Leigh Park – then another and another. So this is why they called Leigh Park the local open prison! I started chatting to the lads I knew. This was going to be OK after all.

The following day I faced the 'reception committee'. First there was the 'thorough' medical check, which was a quick cough and a grope, then being told to clear off. Then I was up in front of one of the governors, who asked me my name and number and told me my release date.

'Outside, Greenaway,' a screw shouted in my ear and I was escorted to my new job of sewing mailbags. The mailbag room was near what we called 'the dolls' house', which was a women's prison. We were paid by how many bags we sewed, and there had to be so many stitches to the inch or they would be slung back at us.

Occasionally a screw would shout out 'visiting magistrate'

and they would come round, asking if anyone had any complaints that they would like to discuss. But who would trust a magistrate? We might end up being grassed up to the screws.

I stole one of the large mailbag needles, heated it up and pushed the hot metal into a broken toothbrush to create a shank – a makeshift weapon. I needed to be tooled up in case of trouble. But it turned out to be an easy sentence. When I was finally released it felt like no big deal. I'd learned nothing, apart from some violent martial arts and defence moves. It became a breeding ground for my anger and made me much worse.

I returned to Leigh Park and met my mate Animal, who told me about a woman called Jackie. Jackie was happy to let our guys call in at any time for coffee and a chat. He thought that she might be willing to take me in as a lodger.

Jackie was a single parent with two sons, living in a small block of flats in the heart of Leigh Park. She didn't hesitate to take me in for the time being, but stressed that I needed to look for somewhere else. Jackie was a diamond, putting up with me and my odd ways. I was able to bring my girlfriends round, and I got on well with the guy she was dating. I ended up becoming her long-term lodger.

In between staying at Jackie's, I spent the next few years touring Her Majesty's 'hotels' including Winchester, Wandsworth, Chelmsford, Exeter, Lewis, Dartmoor and possibly others that I can't remember. It was always for violent offences like grievous bodily harm and wounding with intent. I didn't care. I was like a wild animal.

But wherever I ended up, there were others who were just as insane as I was. Back on remand in Winchester, I was banged up, three to a cell, with a well-known hard guy, who used to walk along the landing head-butting metal doors. I wound him up, saying that anyone could do that once, so he proved me wrong by head-butting a door six times, ending up with blood trickling down his face.

He used to call me the Hilly Billy, because I was a long-haired, rough, country guy. Then one day we started arm-wrestling and I beat him. After that he would come up to me, stroke my arm muscles and say, 'Strong lad.' I had no idea that this hard nut was gay. Eventually I had had enough, and me and my other cellmate tied him up and stuffed a pair of socks in his mouth. He didn't resist.

I rang our cell alarm bell and when the screws came running, they laughed to see this hard man tied up and helpless. More staff gathered to witness this, including an SO (senior officer) who said: 'You know who he is, don't you lad?'

'He's a poof. Get him out of my cell,' I snarled. They untied him and took him away.

Suddenly the SO was in my face. 'Hard man, Greenaway?' he questioned.

I grinned at him and without warning I had a fist in my guts, throwing me across the cell and into the wall. It didn't hurt. I grinned again and the door was quickly slammed in my face. I was marked as an aggressive prisoner and given a single cell.

In Chelmsford I was banged up in a two-up (two in a cell, sometimes known as 'married quarters') with a guy who turned out to be a Satanist. He taught me about the practices of his coven and one day he called up a demon in our cell. Crouched on the floor, shaking and moaning, something appeared in front of us which looked like a huge toad. It's strange how many people I meet nowadays that want to know all the gory details about this incident, but it was a very sinister and nasty experience. To this day I get upset when I see a frog or toad statue because I know it is an occult symbol.

Back then, evil as I was, I was fascinated. He taught me about telepathy and some weeks later, I saw the result. I didn't get many letters or visitors in prison. In fact in one prison I nearly lost it several times with this black lad, also called Greenaway, who would try and grab what few letters I had when our name was called out, so I had to get them quickly. But on this occasion, I was on the other side of the prison from my cellmate when I heard his voice telling me that a letter had arrived for me. He was right, it had. I was blown away. He treated it like it was a normal, everyday event.

But he went too far when he talked about child sacrifices. Prisons are full of storytellers, millionaires and innocent men, so you never know what to believe. But he explained how pregnant women in the coven would be kept hidden, so no one knew about it and then their newborn child was killed in a ceremony, I flew into a rage and wanted to slaughter him. There was little I wouldn't do, but this was beyond my boundaries.

I rang our emergency bell and the screws came quickly. I shoved him out the door as it opened, shouting: 'Get this slag out of my cell or I will kill him!' He was taken away and I never saw him again.

After that I was banged up with a former Coldstream Guard. He's going to be a handy cellmate, I thought.

I was wrong. One evening I was driven mad by a continual thumping above my head. The guys upstairs were doing press-ups, using a chair that was banging down on our ceiling. My anger built up and eventually I flipped and shouted out the window for them to shut up, throwing in a few obscenities and racist insults – they were black guys. Some of the other cons joined in and the noise stopped. Next morning when we were unlocked, I saw a group of black guys coming down the stairs towards me, their faces set in anger. I had just poured a bowl of very hot water to wash myself and as they reached me, I threw it into their faces.

My cellmate saw what happened and I looked to him for support. In disbelief, I watched him run inside our cell and bang the door so that it locked. I was trapped. By now we had attracted the attention of the staff, who knew something was going down. They quickly unlocked the door for me, but I knew I would have to get rid of this tosser – no way was I going to be banged up with someone so gutless.

That lunchtime I saw the same guys moving towards me in the dinner queue. In front of me was a well-known nutter with a psychopathic hatred of other people. I grabbed his shoulder and whispered in his ear: 'Watch out, see those black guys? They're coming for you!' He looked round and saw the angry black guys jumping the queue towards us. With a growing snarl he turned round and flew at them with startling ferocity, smashing his metal tray into them.

I stood back, watching and grinning. He was taken away to the block and later shipped out to some mental hospital. But the black guys never bothered me again.

You always had to keep your eyes open in prison; there was a lot of violence and rivalry, especially if anyone was different. One lad got slashed because he looked a bit too flash and had long blond hair. I knew the London boys didn't like him and one day he came staggering in from the exercise yard. His face had been slashed and he was holding his guts where he had been stabbed.

I did my fair share of troublemaking, though. Sometimes I would shout obscenities at screws in the yard outside my cell window and then quickly duck down. Another time I organised a sit-down strike on the sports field in protest at our poor conditions. (We were often out there watching cons play against outside teams, including the local police. I was tempted to play on our team just to have a chance of crippling the enemy – by accident, of course!)

So on this one occasion we were sat on the field and I passed the word round that we weren't going to go in. There are always a few slags who are too scared to rebel, so when we were summoned back in, half of the group got up and walked inside. I was smug at giving aggro to the screws, until I noticed that our numbers were quickly shrinking. Eventually our group was so small we knew we'd get a good kicking from the growing number of screws gathering, so we gave it up. We were banged up without a word and nothing more was said.

Even inside I still hung around with bikers. Bobby, an Irish guy with slicked-back hair, was one that I met in the sick queue in Chelmsford. I was hoping to get some sort of drugs while Bobby, who was on crutches, was after some pain relief and not too friendly. But we got chatting and he told me that a bus had knocked him off his bike and run him over. We became mates and many years later, I met him again in Northern Ireland – a chance encounter that diffused a potentially dangerous situation.

Conditions inside were always pretty grim. Our cells would be freezing in winter and like an oven in summer. The food was just about bearable, all except for the porridge, which we were told was grade-one, American pig food. The tea was foul and at the bottom of the mug there was always a thick layer of sludge. I've hated tea and porridge ever since.

Between each prison sentence, the violence continued to escalate and so did the paranoia: a knock at the door would always mean either a rival gang with weapons or the police; a car slowing down on the street could be one of either about to grab me. The anger of my past seethed around me like a whirlpool of filth. I had mentally closed up, not letting anyone – even those close to me – get inside my head. I always fought back, armed with weapons and keeping a stash behind the front door for 'visitors', but in reality, I didn't really care what happened to me. Getting hit was like pushing my self-destruct button repeatedly and if I suffered pain, was it any less than I deserved? And if I killed someone, what did it matter?

The police knew that and always checked me out whenever there was a bad stabbing. One day it would all go too far. I tried to get away from it all, but soon found myself handcuffed and escorted by police back to Leigh Park for questioning. I was under arrest for murder.

CHAPTER 5

Killer instinct

Larry King thought of himself as a bit of a ladies' man, a real 'Don Juan' character who actually had the nerve to try it on with my bird! On the day in question, I was walking along with my arm around my long-term girlfriend, when Larry approached her and started chatting her up, right in front of me. This was a real 'red mist' moment. He was going to pay for this!

Later that day, smashed out of my head, I beat up a copper. I knew then that I had to get away from all this insanity. Along with Animal and a couple of young chicks, we fled to Northampton and rented a couple of rooms. One of the girl's parents found out and came to take them home, but I didn't feel I could return to all that trouble. We decided to hang around a bit longer.

Sometime later, back in Leigh Park some kids playing in a local copse had spotted a hand sticking out of the ground. It turned out to be the remains of Larry. He'd been stabbed to death.

The news got back to us about a murder taking place and we decided to try and find out more about it – from the local cop shop, of all places! Staggering in, dirty, unwashed and unfriendly, we growled at the cop behind the desk. Finally he understood what we were trying to ask about.

'Come this way,' he gestured, pointing Animal in one direction, while I was led off in another. We were both questioned and both gave different answers. I was saying: 'Larry King? No, never heard of him.' Meanwhile Animal was telling them: 'Yeah, of course I know him and Brian knows him too.'

We were both arrested for murder and taken, handcuffed, by train back to Leigh Park to be questioned further. I was hoping we could do some winding up on the way home, picking fights with other travellers, but as soon as they saw the handcuffs, they went deaf on us. Changing at Waterloo, we waited in a guarded room for the link train. Animal started messing around with a discarded police helmet, but hearing our laughter, a cop burst in and aggressively snatched it back. When he was told we were being held for murder, he suddenly gulped, looked scared and disappeared.

Some London cops had been brought in by now and one of them had already told me that he didn't think local guys were involved in the murder – he believed it was an outside hit man. The truth was that I had come very close to killing a number of times, which had been one of the reasons I had fled to Northampton to try and stop myself being provoked. But I hadn't killed Larry. However, the fact that I'd given him a good kicking and left him on the floor on the same day that he was murdered was much too close to home.

Eventually we were released without charge. A few days later we spotted some guys we knew working on the road in Havant, digging a hole. I may have been smashed but I could see that one of them was in a really bad place. He looked rough, like he hadn't slept in weeks, and he was really burdened with something. I had always loved people-watching, especially when I was on drugs. I felt that I could almost get into their heads and discern where they were at. At the time I didn't speak to this guy and thought nothing more of it. Later we found out that he was one of the guys convicted with Larry's murder and sentenced to life.

There was one person I became increasingly obsessed with killing: my real dad. I couldn't forget the way he'd abandoned us as children. What made it worse was that a lot of my gang members had lovely parents who supported them, even though some of them spat blood at me because I messed up their kids. The contrast between their life and mine, coupled with years of seething anger and resentment, meant that my hatred grew into something uncontrollable. I had to find him.

I'd heard that he ran a fleet of taxis around Portsmouth train station. I pocketed some weapons and travelled down to Portsmouth with one of my gang. We climbed into the back of a waiting cab.

'Take me to your leader, Greenaway,' I demanded.

'Who are you?' he asked.

'I'm his son.' He looked at me warily, probably guessing that something wasn't right.

'I don't know who you're talking about, mate.' So we left it, but only on this occasion. A Hell's Angel never forgets. If you wronged me, you would pay. And one day I would make sure that he did.

The drugs were slowly destroying me and I took anything I could get my hands on, including acid, which Bobby had introduced me to in Chelmsford. I'd first seen the effects of acid when two lads came out of their prison cell on their hands and knees, barking their heads off, which I thought was hilarious. But under its effects I was now wandering the streets every night on my own, watching the colours swirling around the street lights. I felt that I had nowhere to go and nowhere that I could really call home. Hours later I would come down from the drugs, miles from home, paranoid and ready to attack every passing car that slowed down, thinking they were after me. I was messed up and I knew it. The final time that I was sent down, the judge told me: 'Greenaway, you are hell bent on self-destruction.'

I wanted to yell at him: 'What do you know? What does anyone really know?'

And yet, how right he was.

I knew I needed help. One chance I thought I had was a drug rehab unit in the Portsmouth area, called the Alpha Trust. I had heard that they helped guys like me and I was desperate to sort my head out. But I also heard from others who had been there that you had to knock on the door and virtually beg them to take you in. If you messed up, they made you wear a card around your neck, saying 'I have been a naughty boy'. I didn't know if it was true or not, but I knew that if anyone tried to shame me, I would bust them open.

I did try to get there once, travelling with some mates in a van, until we got pulled over by a pig on a bike. He started questioning some of the other guys and I wandered off to a nearby shop to get some fags. One by one, all my mates wandered off and the cop was left standing on his own at the side of the road. Out of my head as usual, I climbed on a passing bus, watching it all happen as the bus drove away. I have no idea where I ended up.

I remember one morning coming down from drugs and finding myself talking to my doctor in his surgery. I had no idea how I got there. He didn't mince words. 'Brian, if you carry on like this you will be dead in a few months because of the drugs. Either you will OD or be killed while out of your head.'

That did my head in and I walked out of the surgery with tears in my eyes. What he was saying was that I didn't have long to live. What chance did I have? What in the world could possibly change me? I needed the drugs to get me out of the hell of the world that I knew and yet, in truth, my drug world was far worse.

One day, Steve and I were wandering around dressed as 'normal' people. I usually wore my biker gear, which was some filthy, stinking jeans that were never washed, a leather jacket bearing our colours and sometimes a denim sleeveless jacket. But that day, for some odd reason, we decided to be 'civilians'.

We were out of our heads on acid and we ended up walking through a corn field on the edges of Leigh Park. It was pouring with rain and we were soaked to the skin. I remember thinking how wet and cold I would be later on.

On the other side of the field we came to a road where two young girls, about nine or ten years old, were staring at us. Oh no, we had to get away! It was doing my brain in. Taking another look at them, we ran to the other side of the wide road leading into our estate. Steve asked if I wanted to go and meet Graham, who was a bit of a legend on the estate. He had travelled to India on a drugs trail and returned without his brain. I hadn't visited his house before, but looking down the road I saw a house that seemed to radiate warmth and light. I had no idea at that moment how much that visit was going to change my life.

'Is that the house?' I asked. Frowning, Steve said it was. He knew I hadn't been there before. Now all we had to do was to cross the road, which is easier said than done when cars start attacking you! As I edged between two parked cars, they opened their bonnets and snarled at me. I was trapped between them, both growling and snarling at me, their bonnets and boots like huge, open mouths. I had to cross the road quickly before I got eaten. But cars roared past at more than 100mph, followed by the smell of burning rubber and clouds of smoke. The road seemed impossibly wide and getting wider. Our heads were really gone.

Finally arriving at Graham's, there was no answer when we knocked on the door. Wandering round the back of the house, we found a small shed. We knocked at the door, which creaked open slowly and there was the legendary Graham. He looked ancient, had long, thinning blond hair and a stoned expression, although I'd heard he no longer needed drugs because his brain was in such a mess.

Graham gazed at us dreamily and held up his hand. 'Ssh. Can you hear the music?' he whispered.

I could barely make out the sound, but it gradually got louder. I glared at him. Was this guy trying to do my head in? Playing mind games with me was a very dangerous thing to do. But looking down I noticed that Graham had his foot on a pedal and with it was controlling the volume. Cool, I thought.

He took us into the house and we settled in the living room. Graham made himself comfortable on a child's rocking chair and started moving. On one of the rockers he had fixed a musical box, so that each time he moved, the sound kept starting and stopping. Steve sat on my right and started babbling, making lots of meaningless sounds. I felt bad about Steve – he was having a bad trip and it was my fault. I had got him into drugs.

I looked at these two guys – Graham, who was much older than me (or perhaps he just looked it), and Steve, younger than me and a great friend. It was like I was looking at myself in the past and in the future. This is what I started out as and this is what I would become, I thought – permanently out of my head. My life was ruined. I was dead already.

Suddenly there seemed to be a huge sphere hovering in front of me, at least six feet tall, and inside it were lots of square boxes that kept flipping over, like signs at a railway station. Each had a short question written on it like 'Why?' or 'What?' The easiest way to do someone's head in when they are on drugs is to ask questions. They will be struggling to answer the first one while you ask the next one. For a brief moment I felt like I was going into meltdown.

I noticed that there was someone sitting down on the settee near me. He hadn't come in with us and I had no idea who He was. He was giving off a powerful feeling of goodness – a wonderful feeling of love and light radiating out to me. I felt like He cared about me, really loved me and wanted to help me.

I became convinced that this was God. What could I say in the presence of God? Then something came to mind. Many years ago I had attended the Roman Catholic chapel in Chelmsford with my Irish mate, Bobby, who was an RC. Surely if there really was a God, how could He allow this so-called 'religious war' in Northern Ireland to continue? How could He let all this bad stuff happen in His name?

So I started talking to Him, a conversation between us in my drugged-up head. I attempted a challenge.

'You are not who I think You are, are You? If You are who I think You are, what about Northern Ireland?' Now I've got Him, I thought.

But He answered me quickly. 'See that "pot" plant?' He said, pointing to a marijuana plant growing on Graham's windowsill. 'If I cut off the dead branches and leaves, it will give good fruit.' I instantly thought of a tomato plant that you have to trim and prune to get the best tomatoes from it. 'If I leave it, it will be no good.'

This was doing my head in. Here was God and He was speaking to me, Brian Greenaway. No way! I had to tell someone. I immediately thought of Jackie, my landlady. She was straight. She would help me.

I ran most of the way back to the flat and burst in the door, breathless and excited. 'Jackie, Jackie! I've just seen God!'

There was a long pause before she spoke. 'So what were you on?'

My balloon burst. Of course it was the drugs. Stupid me. My shoulders slouched. Why would God bother to speak to me? After all, He knew everything about me. More than anyone, He knew how wicked and evil I was. I was lost for words. I couldn't explain what had just happened. I had believed God had spoken to me, loved me and wanted to give me hope, but reasoning quickly crushed all the good feelings I had felt. I hit rock bottom again.

Sometime later I headed out with the gang one evening to a Roman ruin along a farm track, close to Chichester. We had a load of food and even more drink. Later that evening, two cops arrived and told us they had received complaints about bikes roaring up and down the farm track. They could only see a few of us at this stage. I explained that we hadn't been up and down, that we had just arrived, but clearly they didn't believe me. I was high on drugs and wanted to kill them.

I told them to look around. As they shone their torches, they spotted bike after bike leaning against trees in rows and against each other. They went white – there were loads of us. They left quickly and I thought they were going for more help, but they didn't come back.

Later that evening a couple of 'straight' guys who weren't bikers arrived with their chicks to check us over. One was carrying a double-barrelled twelve-bore shotgun and I followed him around like he was a pool of water in the desert. I really wanted that gun. As they were climbing in and out of the ruins, the armed guy slipped and lost his gun. He couldn't find it and he later disappeared. One of my gang brought it to me, fully loaded.

When I got home, the first thing I did was to cut off the barrels, making them very short. I also cut the stock short too, so that it looked like a big fearful pistol. Previously I had used knives and lumps of steel, but now I had a gun and I carried it everywhere. And the cops never found it. They once stopped and searched me, and I had it tucked down the back of my jeans, broken into three parts so that it wouldn't be spotted.

The monster in me had no boundaries and I was so unpredictable. I must have been doing my mates' heads in because any time they got into an argument with me, I would stick the gun in their face and threaten them. I was out of control. When I chain-whipped a guy in the bus shelter for no reason, I jumped back in my mate's car and we were quickly followed by another car – the people in it had seen what had happened. As they closed in, I thought about shooting at the driver, but instead slid down in my seat, hiding from them. For whatever reason, they pulled back and we heard nothing more.

One evening Animal told us that there was a big barbecue planned in Bognor, so for fun we thought that we would gatecrash the party. About ten of them followed me on my bike, which I parked in a high-walled car park. We had some women with us, so weren't looking for trouble.

While we were hanging about on the beach, someone shouted, 'Skinheads!' We saw them pouring out of a nearby pub, tooled up and ready for a fight. I rubbed my hands together. This wasn't going to be such a bad evening after all!

We headed towards them. More were pouring out, cutting off our retreat. This would be a good battle! We always thought it was better to be well outnumbered, because our story would be so much more dramatic and impressive later. But very quickly I realised that there were too many of them and they would soon overpower us. I shouted to my guys to split.

It was getting dark now. I ran back to the car park, fighting skinheads all the way. A group of them started beating up one of our biker chicks, so I turned back and dived into the fray to deal with them. By the time I got to the car park, most of our guys had their bikes warmed up and ready to go. I ran to my bike and tried to kick-start it, but suddenly realised that I was surrounded by about thirty skinheads. I knew that if I went down, every one of them would want a piece of me and I wouldn't escape alive. Looking up I saw two cops in a police car looking my way, watching but doing nothing. I was on my own.

Suddenly one of the skinheads smashed a cricket bat into my face. I whipped out the stiletto dagger from the inside of my jacket and lashed out at him, stabbing him in the guts. He went down quickly without a sound. Another face was in front of me. I struck out again and he went down. Covered in blood, I ran out of the car park and found my guys, telling one of them to collect my bike and passing my blade to another to hide it. We made our escape, past several police cars hammering past us towards the scene. We thought we'd got away with it, until we came to a police roadblock. I laughed out loud. Just before the police block we spotted a road into a council estate and I shouted to the guys to head that way. Leaping off our bikes, we ran behind a row of garages and hid in the undergrowth. We heard police cars screech to a halt nearby. I told everyone to be quiet.

'Well, they are not here,' I heard a voice say. Car doors slammed and we heard them driving away. They had gone, or so we thought.

Then one of our chicks started giggling. 'Shut up,' I warned. But it was too late. Suddenly a torch shone in our direction. 'Right, you, out. And you! And you!' I could hear the surprise in his voice. He thought he had caught one of us, not a whole group. We were rounded up and taken to a nearby police station.

It was full of skinheads, filling the reception area, lining the corridors and spilling out onto the road. I heard my name repeatedly as I was marched to the interview room, past the jeers and curses. A few tried to kick out at me. I felt very threatened and I knew if that if the roles had been reversed, I would be attacking this guy, not caring about the surrounding police.

The guys I had stabbed were going to die, I was told. They needed emergency surgery and were in intensive care. I laughed. I didn't care.

I was questioned persistently all night. The following morning I was told the skinheads had been rushed back to theatre because they had poison leaking into their guts. My thin blade had stabbed them deeply, puncturing their bowels.

I was held on remand for six weeks and every time I went to the magistrates' court I gave them aggro, almost ripping the door off the box in which we had to sit. I was even more of an animal when escorted by the police. This was the monster at its worst. I cared about nothing and no one, and didn't give a toss what happened to me.

Both Animal, myself and a few others did our remand in Winchester. I still had an intense loathing for screws and played with the emergency bell in my cell to wind them up. But then one of the lads I was banged up with had a raging toothache and needed help. I rang and rang. No answer. I carried on relentlessly until two screws appeared, red-faced and fuming. I told them it was genuine this time, but they dragged me down the block. I knew that whenever anyone was nicked and taken to the block, they could expect trouble, so I watched them all the way, waiting for them to start on me. I was thrown into an empty, filthy cell. The mattress stank of urine, and it was wet and cold. The door slammed shut and I waited. I knew I was in for a kicking.

A bit later I heard movement outside my cell. They were going to come in on me, team-handed – with a mattress in front of them so I couldn't get at them – and 'do me' with their sticks. There was nothing I could do but wait. Then I heard them talking about my going to court the next day and how they couldn't get away with injuring me, so they decided not to bother.

On 23 January 1973 I was sentenced to four years for various offences including causing an affray, unlawful wounding, carrying offensive weapons, damaging a police cell and driving while disqualified. It totalled twelve years on paper, but the sentences ran concurrently (served at the same time). Animal went down for eighteen months and the others got suspended sentences, including one of our gang who had grassed us up to the police. Being the leader, I was hit the hardest. I was told that it was a waste of time trying to appeal and I knew that was right.

Early the next morning in Winchester I was told to pack my kit. I must be off to another wing, I thought. Wrong. I was being ghosted out, that is sent to another prison with no warning. They clearly didn't want me there.

Eight of us were handcuffed and sat away from each other in the prison van. We drove for miles and along the way, six were dropped off in Dorset. I still had no idea where we were going, until we stopped off in Exeter overnight, where I found out about the awful place where I was to spend the next four years of my life. I would be leaving a very different person to the one I'd been when I went in.

CHAPTER 6

Light in the darkness

'Oh I hear you're going to Dartmoor,' a screw said to me as I got ready to leave Exeter. 'That will wake you up, lad. That will teach you.' I had heard about the reputation of the 'Moor', where in those days some of the most dangerous and evil prisoners were kept, but I just grinned at him. This was just another prison to me.

For the last few miles of the journey, I looked out of the window at the bleak landscape. Dartmoor, in the West Country, is nearly 400 square miles of bogs, swamps and open moorland. It was desolate, huge and barren. But I didn't give a damn. They could do what they wanted. They would never break me.

The prison, in Princetown, was halfway up a hill next to what looked like a small village, which I later found out were screws' houses. Driving through the gate, I realised that this was like no other prison I had been in. Black granite buildings were scattered across a vast space, surrounded by a high fence and patrolled by guards and their dogs. The bus stopped to allow a working party of cons to pass. They had hardened, hostile faces and suddenly one of them, a real head-banger, pointed at us and doubled up laughing. At first I wanted to rip his throat out, but then fear hit me for the first time. Was that what this place did to cons, drive them nuts? Was that how I was going to end up? I started to shake.

The next day, after going through the usual reception rubbish again, I was taken in to see the chaplain. I took an instant dislike to him. He was sitting behind a table looking at me, with cigarette ash all down the front of his black shirt.

'Do you want a smoke?' he asked, offering me his full tin of tobacco. Smokes are currency in prison, so I tried to cram as much as I could into a cigarette paper.

'OK if I keep it for later, sir?' That would make at least four prison smokes. What a sucker!

'So what are you going to do when you get out?' he asked. What? He'd obviously got me mixed up with someone else.

'But I'm a reception prisoner, just starting a four.'

'Yes, yes I know, but what are your plans for your release?' He's having a laugh! I told him that if he spoke to me again in the prison, I would sort him out and I stormed out, foaming at the mouth. Still, I'd got a good smoke in my pocket, so perhaps it had been worth it.

I was told that I would be working in the TV shop. This sounded more interesting than my last few prison jobs. Perhaps I would learn how to repair them. I was taken to the workshop where I looked around for the TVs. All I could see were tables with piles of small plastic fittings, each with twelve holes. All we were doing was fitting different-coloured wires into each hole. Around each table were cons working away. They looked like they had switched their brains off. I was going to be one of them.

The only time they came to life was when there was a fight. The first time I saw this happen, the instructor pressed the alarm and a horde of crazy screws burst into the room and dragged the fighters apart. I soon learned to get out of the way fast to avoid being trampled. Prison officers beating cons as they led them away was all par for the course. Perhaps being so far away from anyone, they believed they could get away with it.

Because the prison was halfway up a hill, I thought that the clouds must have got tired of the steep climb and decided to chuck rain at us all the time. There was a joke that you could always tell when a guy had done 'bird' (doing time) in Dartmoor because he had webbed hands! It was a place of constant bad weather, where one minute it would be sunshine and the next a full blown storm.

As a result of all the rain, there was a very expensive, porous exercise yard which didn't flood and dried out quickly. But we still had to walk around inside the wings when it rained. In the rare good weather, we were out in the yard, where I would watch the men wandering round. I'd got to know a few of them and knew what they were in for. A lot of them were in for murder and yet they weren't anywhere near as bad as me. I remember a Welsh guy who had hit another guy against the wall in a fight accidentally cracking his skull and killing him. That could have been me so many times over. I thought that I was destined to spend the rest of my life in and out of prison, with the sentences getting longer each time, until I lost my sanity and they 'nutted' me off to Broadmoor Hospital as a mental patient.

To help sort my head out, I was sent to see a psychiatrist, who came highly recommended. I'd seen shrinks before for pre-sentence reports, but I really felt that they didn't understand where I was coming from. Perhaps this one would be different. But when I first saw her, it blew me away. She was old, wearing a very short skirt and long thigh-length boots. I later heard rumours that guys had scored with her. How the heck was she going to help me? Look at the state of her! I started to see her every week, but the more I saw her, the less it helped, so I stopped going.

I decided to go on a City and Guilds building course, learning about bricklaying, mixing mortar, roofing and drains. I thought the trainer was an idiot, though. He boasted about a mistake he had made in a building when he was an engineer in Plymouth. It could still be seen to this day. How could you boast of cocking something up? I still had a love of watching men take pride in their work and do a good job, so he really wound me up. I don't know if I learned anything really valuable and we never got our certificates, but at least on the works' department the screws would leave you alone for most of the time.

Meanwhile I was marking off my bird in an exercise book. I had marked in squares to represent each day inside, and every night I went through the ritual of crossing off a day. This was called doing bird the hard way because they slide by so slowly. Dartmoor was not a place that anyone in their right mind would want to be, but there was no escape. I often looked at the granite wall outside, thinking it wasn't that high. But we'd heard stories of guys who had tried to escape. The other side of the wall had pillars built into it called back-breakers, because if you slid down the wall, they would immediately break your spine. And then there were the moors to get through. No one had ever managed that.

Later I was given a job with more trust and responsibility, just me and a civilian electrician called Tony. He was a young man who never gave me any hassle and seemed to get a buzz out of working with a Hell's Angel president. However, he once got a real telling off from the security staff. He had let me walk behind him, carrying a ladder. One swing with it and I could have knocked him out and then used the ladder to scale the wall.

It's a good job the screws didn't see me holding him against the wall on the day the 'vampires' came! The local blood donation team were looking for volunteers and I wanted to put my name down. I occasionally enjoyed doing something good – not that I wanted to ruin my hard reputation by telling anyone. A Hell's Angel geezer giving blood – no way!

I talked Tony into coming with me and, trying to be tough, I said afterwards that we didn't need to sit down with tea and biscuits to get our strength back. But as soon as we got outside, Tony collapsed. I quickly grabbed him and held him against the wall, trying to get him to stand. I knew that if the screws appeared they would think I had hit him and be all over me like a sweaty blanket. Fortunately, no one saw us.

It felt like the screws were always on our backs, using any excuse they could to fly at us. Sometimes they would do things just to wind us up. During association, when we were let out of our cells each evening for leisure time, we could be five minutes away from the end of a TV programme when a screw would come over and turn it off. I could have easily slammed him with my chair.

I remember one night we were banged up and I heard someone shouting downstairs. It became more heated and I heard the sounds of running and keys jangling. Suddenly the screws were beating someone up and we could clearly hear every blow. A few of us started shouting obscenities, but when the beatings stopped, I heard some of the doors being unlocked and guys being smacked. I could be next. I sat down quickly on my bed and tried to look innocent.

One evening a short, stocky prisoner asked me if I wanted to play table tennis with him. Anything was better than being banged up. After a while one of the more hated screws beckoned me over. I knew I was in trouble.

'Do you know who that is you're playing table tennis with, Greenaway?' he asked.

I had no idea. It turned out that he wasn't just another con; he was a serious sex offender, known as the 'beast of Dartmoor'. Nonces (sex offenders) were hated in prison.

'If I see you with him again, you're for it,' he growled.

The next evening, I'd forgotten about the warning and played another game with him. The same screw called me over. I could see that he was steaming.

'I warned you yesterday, Greenaway,' he yelled at me. I knew then that I would need to keep an eye on this one – he wanted my guts. But in the end I heard no more from him.

We had a probation officer in Dartmoor called Tony Sykes. He was one of the few good and genuine staff members, and I found out much later that he was a Christian. He didn't talk about his beliefs, but just got on with helping men sort their lives out.

After some months Tony came to my cell and asked if I would like to have a prison visitor. He had heard that a group of my friends had come to see me stoned out of their heads. They had threatened the screws and been turned away. Nobody else had come to visit me. He told me about someone called Martin Gough, a farmer who lived in nearby Tavistock. Tony told me that Martin's son was into bikes, so we would have something in common to talk about.

'But I don't want to talk about bikes, I want to talk about God,' I told him. Blimey, where did that come from? I hadn't planned to say it. I had no idea at this time that Tony was a Christian, but there were all sorts of 'God things' going round my head by now and I was desperate to sort them all out.

I had always believed that there was a God. Looking at how beautiful and awesome nature was – something I had always loved since childhood – I knew that it had to be God's hand. But God was for nice people and I was a rat bag. Why would God want to know me? Hadn't my mum drummed it into me that I was no good and I was going to hell?

At this point in my life I really was at the end of my tether. There was nowhere else to go and if God couldn't help me, then nobody could. I was finished. I would end up killing someone or being killed.

I'd been to prison chapels a few times, just to get out of my cell. Once in Winchester, I remember the chaplain's Bible reading was from 1 Corinthians 13, something about God's love. At the time it had knocked me for six, because it spoke volumes, even though I had no love in me. While in Dartmoor I wouldn't go near the Church of England chapel because of my hatred for the chaplain I had met at reception, so I attended the Methodist chapel instead. The Methodist chaplain seemed very genuine and I had a lot of respect for him. I used to grab all the literature I could, just to have something to read when I went back to my cell, something that might just keep the crap out of my brain.

When Martin came to see me, I met him in what appeared to be a large classroom with a glass door. The screw sat respectfully outside. Martin was and still is a special man. He was great with me and we talked for a long time, maybe an hour. I can't remember what we talked about, but at the end he asked me if there was anything he could get for me. A million thoughts flashed through my mind: a nice large house near Torquay, a boat, loads of money! Suddenly I remembered the *Methodist Recorder* – a newspaper from the chapel that I had been reading. On the back page there was always an advert for The Living Bible. The way it was explained made me feel that this Bible was written for street guys, so even idiots like Brian Greenaway could read and understand it! I had tried reading bits of the Bible in prison before, but it was always from the King James version, which may as well have been in Latin for all that I could understand. It didn't touch me in any way.

'Have you heard of The Living Bible?' I asked Martin.

He smiled, reached into his briefcase and pulled out two paperback books. One was The Living Bible, exactly like I had seen in the advert in the *Methodist Recorder*. That blew me away. The other was a blue book with a picture of a stiletto dagger on the front cover, just like the one I had stabbed the skinheads in Bognor with.

'I thought you might like to read these,' he said. Amazing!

The books were handed to a screw, so they could be checked for hidden drugs or anything else. That was standard procedure. But they were given back to me with no comment the next day. That was rare.

Alone in my cell, I looked at the book with the knife on the front. This had to be interesting, I thought. The book was called *Run Baby Run*, and was about Nicky Cruz, a Puerto Rican New York gang leader. As I read, it felt like I was reading about myself, but it was in New York instead of Leigh Park. And then it talked about Nicky being changed from a vicious gang leader to a Christian by crying out to God, being filled with His love and forgiven for all the bad things he had done. I was blown away.

I knew deep down that this was true because I could feel God in it all. My eyes blurred as the tears flowed. I never cried. I was too hard to cry. Men don't cry. I would get my head kicked to pieces and I wouldn't cry. Bad things would happen around me and I wouldn't cry. But, as I was reading this book, I couldn't stop crying. We all had single cells in Dartmoor and I didn't have to tolerate the lack of privacy and going to the toilet in front of another prisoner. But I had never been more grateful for a single cell than at that moment!

Nicky wrote about Jesus coming into his life. Where could I find this Jesus? Nicky's nightmare had stopped. Where could I find a preacher to tell me about this love of God and this Jesus who changes lives? Then I remembered The Living Bible. I picked it up. I had no idea where to start reading, so I just let the pages fall open and read what was in front of me. It was John's Gospel and it said:

'I am the true Vine, and my Father is the Gardener. He lops off every branch that doesn't produce. And he prunes

those branches that bear fruit for even larger crops. He
has already tended you by pruning you back for greater
strength and usefulness by means of the commands I gave
you. Take care to live in me, and let me live in you. For a
branch can't produce fruit when severed from the vine. Nor
can you be fruitful apart from me.' (John 15:1–4, TLB)

I was moved to tears again. This was what the man I believed
was God had said to me that day when I was out of my head on
acid with Steve and Graham. I had thought it was the drugs.
Jackie had thought it was the drugs. But it can't have been. If
God was who He said He was, then surely He could choose to
speak to us in any state of mind? I've since met other Christians
who have had similar experiences. But I knew right then and
there that He was speaking to me. If I wanted to have a good and
fruitful life it was right there on offer.

It was about 8pm by now, the day after my birthday in 1973.
As I lay on my bed facing the door, it was as though God had
walked into my cell. I couldn't see Him, but I knew that He was
with me. I cried uncontrollably.

'Please God, come into my life and help me to change, just like
You did for Nicky,' I cried. 'Please forgive me.' I wondered if I was
saying the right things, but God knew my heart and He knew
how much I desperately wanted to change, to have a life worth
living and to be a different person from the maniac that I was.

Suddenly it was as though there was a hole in my skull where
God was pouring His love into me and holes in my feet where
all the garbage that had been Brian Greenaway was being taken
away. I felt completely forgiven. But it was more than that. I was
twenty-seven years old and for the first time in my life, I felt
loved. It was so powerful, so immense, so immeasurable! He
loved me – knowing all that I had done, knowing how I had
fought my insanity – and still He loved me. I had known hatred

to the depths of my soul, but love was completely foreign to me and it was wonderful.

I had to tell someone about this. In fact, I had to tell the whole world!

The next morning when the screws came along banging on the doors and shooting open our locks, I dashed into the cell next door to see my mate Carl.

'Hey Carl! Carl, guess what? God loves you!' He looked back at me as though I had blown a gasket.

One thing that being the president of the Hell's Angels had given me was a big mouth. Maybe I got some of it from my dad who I was told had been a regimental Sergeant Major in the army. But now I used my big mouth to tell everyone I knew in the prison about God. It was like being in love and wanting to shout it from the rooftops. They couldn't handle it. Greenaway, a Christian? No way! Surely he was this tough guy glaring and growling at everyone? Now suddenly he's talking about the love of God!

Not surprisingly many thought I had finally lost it through drugs. Others thought that I was trying to get parole (early release). But I didn't care what they thought about me. What mattered was that I didn't let God down. I desperately needed to tell them. They could have kicked me to pieces, but I still had to tell them. Nothing in this world could stop me telling people and it never will.

I really related to a story in the Bible about Jesus healing a man who had been blind since birth. I don't believe the blind man would just say, 'Oh, thank you very much.' Surely he would be shouting his head off in excitement: 'Yes, I can see! Thank you, Jesus!' That's how I felt. How could I sit still and keep quiet and continue acting as though nothing had happened? I finally had a father who loved me. The only dad I had known up until then had blanked me, and my stepfather had no idea about how to be a dad and was just there to beat me into shape. But now I had a Dad who had cleaned me up from all the filth I was in and valued me more than anything. I felt so different. Everything looked different; clean, fresh and sparkling. Even the huge granite blocks that formed the prison buildings shone like marble. It felt like I was living in a palace. It all looked so beautiful.

However, it meant that I became about as popular as AIDS. Quickly the other lads knew that I would start trying to tell them about God whenever I came near them, and I was shunned by everyone. Some cons who were prison grasses used to put messages in the letter collection boxes saying that I was up to something. This meant that I got regular visits from the 'burglars', the security staff who would search me and spin my cell, looking for anything suspect. It really wound me up at first and then it just became amusing.

The electrician I worked with, Tony, had no escape, because he had to keep me close to him at all times. I even prayed for him and his wife when they were having a tough time. He couldn't cope with that. He had enjoyed working with a Hell's Angel president, but suddenly I was a Christian and saying: 'Tony, I'm just going to pray about this now.' I could feel him shrinking away from me in embarrassment.

Not long after all this happened I had a visit from a Christian probation officer who had heard about my new faith. As I told her what had happened, she suddenly became excited. 'What day did this happen?'

I told her and she frantically searched through her diary. She found the day I had become a Christian. She explained that she had been up to the prison that day and on the road home, she felt God was telling her to pray. She didn't know why, but she prayed and God had acted.

There was only one other Christian in the prison that I knew about, who was on my wing, but we were from different backgrounds and didn't mix much. But Tony, the probation officer, spent a lot of time with me chatting and praying for me. He really helped me in those early months of being a Christian.

We had regular concerts put on for us in Dartmoor and on one occasion, the Church of England chaplain that I didn't like stood up at the start and told us that he was retiring. I leapt to my feet cheering and shouting myself hoarse, as did most of the other guys in the room. It hit him hard. His face was white and he looked shocked. He must have known how people felt towards him. I had a lot of respect for the honest and genuine figures of authority and in the church, but he was more interested in keeping in with screws and cadging their drinks.

We soon had a new chaplain, Noel Proctor, who became very well-known in Christian circles and wrote a number of books. Much later he was the chaplain in Strangeways Prison at the time of the riots in 1990.

However, I had no time for him at first, but I watched him from a distance. Now I have never had a memory for names, but in a matter of just a few weeks Noel was chatting to prisoners and knew all their first names. That blew me away. A while later, we heard that there was going to be a Christmas concert and the screws had demanded that it was kept for them and their families and not for the cons, because there weren't enough staff members available on the day. We understood that Noel said: 'No prisoners, no concert.' That won us over to him. I knew that he was a good guy and started to go to his events. He held a midweek group and a load of us would go over to the chapel, usually wound up with various bad things that had happened to us throughout the day. We would go and sing our heads off and in between, Noel would tell us his best jokes. We came out feeling a million times better. He was a real blessing to us.

Doing bird as a Christian in Dartmoor was tough, but there was one period when the pressure was taken off. I was shipped out to the surgery unit at Grendon Prison, in Grendon Underwood, to have some tattoos removed. I had the word 'HATE' tattooed on my left hand and things like swastikas around my wrist that I had asked to be removed. When I arrived, the other guys were out on exercise, so I started reading my Bible. When they came back and saw me, they asked me what I was reading. That set me off! Out of the six guys on the ward, I led four of them to Christ. But one of them, who didn't want to know at the time, later faced the consequences of his unchanged life. I met him years later in Winchester where he finally became a Christian. But by then he was serving a life sentence for killing his cousin. How different things could have been for him.

In one of the nearby single cells was a young, pimply lad of about nineteen. He had committed a serious sex offence and murdered his victim. The guys made up their minds to give him a kicking. At one time I would have joined in, but I asked the guys to cool it and let me have a word with him.

I visited him in his cell and sat on his bed. I told him that we knew who he was and what he had done and that the others wanted to beat him up. But I also told him that I was a Christian and he, as much as anyone, needed Jesus to help sort out the mess that his life had become. He was too afraid to respond and he later disappeared. It had to be his choice at the end of the day, as with anyone I speak to. Once I've done my bit, it's between them and God.

My faith had transformed my life and outlook in so many ways, but part of the old me still remained. I found out just how controlling it still was when an incident happened that left me shocked and ashamed. Despite having the love of God in me, I was fully prepared to commit murder.

CHAPTER 7

Facing reality

It was very common in Dartmoor for us to have our own budgie for company in our cells. I cared very much about my bird. He would come over and attack my pen when I was writing or drawing, as though asking for my attention and I would play with him. It may sound a bit sad, but for a lot of us it was the only thing we could show any emotion to. At times when we were unlocked, guys would come out onto the landing and budgies would fly about, having their daily exercise, before returning to their owners.

One cold winter day I came back to my cell and the door was open. I looked inside and saw that my bird was missing. Whenever I went to work, I secured his cage door with a small piece of wire because he had learned how to push it open and escape. But now the door was wired open. I looked at the window, which I had left open, with protective mesh covering the gap. The mesh had been thrown to the floor. My bird, used to the warmth of my cell, had flown out into the freezing cold and would never survive. I totally lost it. I ran to a nearby screw, Bert, one of the few that I liked.

'Who was on bars and windows today?' I asked him breathlessly, struggling in anger to get my words out. An officer would check our doors and windows every day to see if they were secure and hadn't been tampered with. Bert pointed across the landing to a little Scottish screw that I hated. He was a gutless bully, hiding behind his uniform and always stood behind others. He was watching me.

'Right,' I snarled and headed for him. I would teach him to fly! He was going over the banisters, no matter what. I was so furious that you could have hit me repeatedly with the cosh that screws carried to control prisoners, but it wouldn't have stopped me. Bert quickly pulled me back by my collar.

'Get in your cell, now,' he shouted at me. I was left to try and calm down, and then Bert came back later and told me to go and get my dinner. All the other guys had gone and I was the only one out, still pumping with adrenalin and anger. Bert followed me down and came back to my cell with me.

'So what was all that about, then?' I pointed to my empty bird cage and told him what had happened. Looking straight in my face, Bert asked me: 'And what were you going to do? Were you really willing to throw everything away and kill him over a budgie?'

It felt like he had pulled me up by my throat and reality hit me. Was I mad? Could I really have done that? And I called myself a Christian? I was suddenly eaten up with shame over what had happened. But it also scared me because I suddenly realised that the old Brian Greenaway had come back. I knew that if I was confronted by this officer, I would want to rip his throat out. But the Scottish screw suddenly disappeared completely from the wing. So even though I felt that I'd blown it and let down all these guys that I'd told about Jesus, God would not let me hurt this officer. I believe God overruled and kept the guy away from me. Many times over in my Christian life since, my temper has flared up and God has intervened in some way to stop me losing it completely.

The following few weeks were hard. I was upset over losing the budgie, which had sometimes seemed to be the only friend I had. It hadn't been my first pet. We had dogs once in childhood, but they died. I think I would have turned out very differently if they had lived. I would have had something to care for, something that loved me. To try and make me feel better, one of the other prisoners managed to get me another budgie, but it was never the same.

More than anything, I was upset and deeply ashamed that I'd lost it again.

Bert, the prison officer, didn't believe I was a Christian after that, because he had seen this insanity rise in me. Years later, I met him at Wellingborough Prison, Northamptonshire. I was a visiting evangelist and I knew that he was working there. Outside in the car park I prayed for a chance to speak to him and as soon as I arrived at the gatehouse, there was Bert alone, ready to book me in. I was finally able to talk to him and explain about that incident.

One of the first lessons that I learned back then was that it's pretty easy to become a Christian and accept God's forgiveness and love, but living the Christian life is tough. I also learned that it was all too easy to make mistakes and get it wrong. What made it worse was that everyone was watching me.

Before I was a Christian, being brutal to someone was easy, but now even swearing was something that I would be very ashamed of. I found it hard to stop and whenever I swore, there was always someone willing to point the finger and say, 'Christians don't swear.' How did they know? They were the same as I had been and I had no idea what Christians did and didn't do. If only they had known how desperately I wanted to get it right.

I felt totally alone with my faith at this time, but God really lifted me up and strengthened me, reassuring me that He wasn't going to blow me out or turn His back on me, even when I was hurting, alone, angry or making mistakes.

I still had the support of Martin Gough, Tony Sykes the probation officer and the chaplain, Noel. In fact, we found out through the prison grapevine that Noel's wife was ill with cancer, and yet he still had time for us!

Noel arranged some Bible study courses for me. I felt like a piece of blotting paper, with such a thirst for knowledge about God. I had the help of a really good tutor, who was always interested in my work and became a good friend.

Yet there was another problem. I was now studying in my cell instead of going down in association to watch TV or to get into trouble for talking to the wrong prisoner. One evening two officers came to my cell and gleefully told me that they had written me down as anti-social. Were they having a laugh? It seemed that whatever I did, it would be wrong. There was no way of pleasing them.

One day an officer came to me with a parole application for potential early release. This had to be another joke! The last time I was given parole papers I hadn't even bothered to look at them; there was no way I would get parole because of my history of violence. Now I thought that it might just be worth the aggravation of filling in the forms, even though I still didn't believe it could happen.

I soon forgot about it and got on with my prison life. But those last six months were very hard. I'd had about a year of trying to talk to everyone about God, with very few responding, and I felt like I was the only believer in the world. I felt totally alone. I got comfort from reading my Bible, especially about others who had been in the same situation. However, it was a dark time of depression – one of many I would struggle with in the years ahead.

Eventually my parole results came back and I'd been given five months early release. I was stunned. Such things don't usually happen in Dartmoor. What seemed strange was that I'd also applied to join the prison outside works' party, but that was refused. Why didn't they trust me to work outside the prison, yet they trusted me with parole?

Much later Martin told me that the governor had said: 'I've seen many men in prison get religion, but there's something different about Greenaway.' That meant a lot to me. No way was I going to break that trust because if I did, it would mess it up for many others like me. If I became another negative statistic and ended up back inside, it could stop others getting early release.

One of the conditions was that I stayed at the Coke Hole Trust in Andover, Hampshire. It was a drug rehab that I had been in touch with whilst in prison. I was free from drugs, but this was run by Christians and I wanted to be around other believers.

On my release day, I dressed in my normal clothes again, gathered my few belongings and my luggie, and walked through the huge gates to wait for my taxi. I breathed in deeply. So this was it freedom! I had been a very different person when I entered Dartmoor. It was a hard prison, but because of what happened to me when I met with God, it has always remained a special place.

There were two of us released that morning and we were escorted by taxi to Plymouth railway station. We soon picked out the plain-clothed cop in the crowds. He was easy to spot. There was a kind of intensity about his casualness! They were usually sent to keep an eye on us to see that we left properly, didn't hang around the prison and didn't cause any problems in the excitement of our new-found freedom. I didn't feel excited. But I was starting to worry about my future. I had been back inside too many times. What if it was a hard habit to break? The slow train to Andover gave me plenty of time to think. Usually on my release, I had wanted to run home, wherever home was. But I was in no hurry this time.

I was picked up from Andover railway station and taken to the Coke Hole Trust. The Trust had separate male and female hostels, and I was taken to the male one, St Vincent's House.

The setting was wonderful. Tucked away at the end of a long country lane, away from crowds and noise, the house had a long veranda and was set in grounds with an overgrown copse and a nearby pond. Four other guys with long drug histories, like me were staying there.

My budgie was taken away and I never found out where it went. I was told that pets weren't allowed. I hadn't been too attached to it anyway. But instead of a budgie, I soon had a dog to fuss over. This big brown 'bear' – a Newfoundland dog with a thick, shaggy coat and a wonderful temperament – would greet us every time we went outside.

I was told I had to stay on site for the first month. I had to conform and know my boundaries, which was tough. I was never any good at taking orders and still struggled with authority, which pressed all the wrong buttons.

The day after my arrival Paul, the house parent, asked me if I fancied a trip to London. Of course I did! I had been banged up for years. One of the other residents, Tony, had gone away for a weekend and ended up back on drugs. Five days later he had phoned, needing help.

I expected Paul to want to rush out straightaway and make a dash to London, but he was really chilled out and we went much later in the day. When we arrived somewhere in London, we went straight to where Tony said he would be. He had phoned hours ago and I was convinced he would have moved on by then.

We found him crashed out against some railings and we managed to get him into the car. Tony seemed to be out of it, not really even knowing who Paul was, but he suddenly looked at me and said, 'Are you Brian Greenaway?' I was gobsmacked. He had never met me before. Paul later explained that they had talked to the guys a lot about me before I arrived.

We returned to the home of the Trust directors Barbara and Doug Henry. Tony was in a bit of a state and he was taken into a bathroom to be cleaned up. I sat with them, watching Barbara and Doug talk gently to Tony as they cleaned him up. I was so moved. It was like watching a mum and dad caring for a wayward son. I had tears in my eyes that I didn't want anyone to see. Here was this junkie that they had been helping, and he had let himself and them down. But there was no slagging off, just loving a guy who seemed unlovable and was loveless. It was a privilege to witness real Christian love. They were very special people.

We always met at Barbara and Doug's house on Sunday evening with the residents of the female hostel, and I also started attending a local Baptist church, where I was baptised. What always surprised me was that there was a large congregation on Sundays with several hundred people, but when I attended the midweek prayer meeting there were about eight attending. Where was everyone? I was confused. Before my release I had read in my Bible about the new Church and got really excited. I believed I was going to go out into this wonderful, beautiful church where everybody loves Jesus, were really good to each other and totally committed to God and His Church ... I was really disappointed at first and thought I must have misunderstood what I had read. But then reality hit me. I soon learned that Christians were just like me – they make mistakes and don't always do what they know they should.

It took me weeks to pluck up enough courage to pray in front of other people. I was so nervous about getting it wrong and I was worried they would think I would start swearing. Despite my struggles when I was banged up, I never swore in front of them.

I soon got work at a metal die-casting firm, pouring molten metal from the furnace into moulds. It was a good job, but I often felt like I was the one melting from the heat. I also had some great leisure time and one thing I enjoyed was canoeing on a local river with one of the staff members. It was good fun and I usually managed to overturn the canoe and soak us both.

But he never moaned about it and he was a wonderful guy.

I started going out with Barbara and Paul to churches and colleges to give talks about the work of the Trust, which I really enjoyed. Paul even took me back to Leigh Park to talk to some old friends. I bumped into my old mate Animal who was working on a really flash chopper.

As I was admiring his wheels, he said, 'Do you want to take it for a ride, Brian?' Is the Pope a Catholic? Of course I wanted to! But I knew that as soon I was on a bike with no insurance or licence, the police would have bounced all over me: 'Got you again, Greenaway!' Without the initial support of the Trust as a stepping-stone into my new life as a Christian, there may have come a time when I would have given in to temptation, surrounded by old mates who were still villains.

I was still at risk of losing my temper. Once on the estate when I had a drink with some of my old mates, I was being threatened by someone in the bar. When we came out we were having a laugh about it, but I was seriously tempted to go back and deal with him. My mates persuaded me to leave it. How quickly the old Brian Greenaway could still leap to the front, even when it was no big deal.

While I was in Leigh Park it was important to me that I visited Jackie, my old landlady. I knew that she wasn't too keen to see me; she was fed up and angry with me being in and out of prison. When I arrived at her flat and knocked on the door, she shouted, 'Come in.' She didn't even know that it was me!

'Jackie, it's Brian,' I shouted to her as I walked in, waiting for her to throw me out – she had every right to. But she didn't. She looked really bad. Her face was battered and bruised, and she had black eyes. She explained that she had been in an accident while driving a newspaper delivery van and had gone through the window. She was pleased to see me and I couldn't wait to tell her about my new life.

'Jackie, you remember when I told you I saw God? You thought it was the drugs, but it was for real!' I told her what had happened to me in Dartmoor and I am sure that my face showed it. She reached out and filled the kettle and continued to make coffee for us both while I talked about God. Before the kettle had finished boiling, Jackie had prayed with me and asked Jesus to come into her life. She knew me so well, had seen the change in me and wanted the same for herself.

I lost touch with Jackie after that because I needed to keep away from Leigh Park in general to avoid my old enemies. I heard years later that she had died. I didn't know how it had happened. I remember that after her road accident, she said that she felt lucky to be alive. Maybe God had preserved her life back then so that I could have a chance to tell her about Jesus. I was so glad I had that opportunity.

I was with the Coke Hole Trust for about five months and when I left, I moved to Woodfalls on the western edge of the New Forest. I found a job I enjoyed, working in precision engineering. However, I felt guilty about keeping my past hidden and felt I had to come clean with the boss and tell him I was an ex-con. As far as he was concerned, I worked hard and kept my nose clean. What went on outside of the factory was my business. He was a good man.

However, his wife was a bit nervous of me because of my background, even though she was a nice Christian lady. Their son sometimes worked in the factory, sitting near me and she would walk by looking at us with a worried expression. But in reality all I wanted was to talk to her son about Jesus. I would sit at my drilling machine chatting to him about the change God had made in my life. In the end he became a Christian and there were times when I was invited to join my boss and his family for a meal at their home.

After some months I began to get restless. I had a real sense that God was calling me to attend Bible college. How could someone like me manage that? I was so thick, I was condensed! But I was passionate about learning more. Then one day in the church I had started attending, there was a visiting speaker who talked about some 'rough diamond' in his church with a colourful background like mine, who was now at Bible college. That was enough for me. If he could do it, then so could I.

I explained my plan to my boss and he told me that he didn't want to lose me. He said if I was to stay with him, he would look after me. Even though giving up a good job to become a student was a risk, I was determined to do what I believed God wanted me to.

I spoke to people at church and got their support, and attended an interview at Moorlands Bible College (now Moorlands College) in Sopley, Christchurch – a beautiful old building, with some additional cabin classrooms.

I was nervous going to the interview, especially when I was shown into a big office, where the principal and two tutors were sat behind a large desk looking at me. This wasn't good. It was like I was up in court again. How on earth would they accept me? I understood that you needed to have several 'O' levels to get in and I had nothing, not even a 'Z' level! But if God wanted it to happen, I was sure it would.

The principal at the time was Dr Derek Copley, a scientist who wrote a book called *Building with Bananas*, about odd characters in the Church. He was into odd people like me and he seemed to like me very much. So after I had been working for about a year, Moorlands contacted me to say that I had a place there if I wanted it. I was delighted, yet anxious. I hadn't been in a classroom since school and even then I didn't pay much attention. It was going to be tough. I had a lot of catching up to do.

— CHAPTER 8 —

Educating Brian

Travelling to Moorlands was going to be a challenge. How on earth would I manage a fifty-mile round trip every day without transport? I prayed about it and one day, one of the church members approached me.

'I've got a motorbike,' he said. 'Do you want to use it for the journey?' My ears pricked up.

'Cor, yeah! What an answer to prayer!' And then I went to collect it. My heart sank. It was a little Honda 49cc. Well, at least it was better than walking.

The journey to college each day was a huge embarrassment. Here was I, an ex-Hell's Angel president used to tearing up the open road with my gang on huge powerful bikes, now struggling on this little 'bicycle' that could barely get up a hill! I had to pedal it to get it started and it would be flat out doing 30mph if I was lucky. When it spluttered up steep slopes, I had to pedal it again to get some power behind it. Lorries would thunder past me and the gust of wind would blow me into the hedge. It was so humiliating. I used to pray: 'Please God, don't let anyone see me on this!' At least my ex-Hell's Angels' mates didn't roar past me on their bikes. I definitely would have ended up in the ditch then.

Arriving at college, often soaking wet from thin 'waterproof' gear that let the rain in, I hid the bike behind the massive laurel bushes surrounding the grounds, hoping no one would find out I had arrived on it. What a way to learn humility!

When I first started attending college, I was met by one of the senior students who took me for a hot drink to thaw me out. We had a brief time of prayer before starting classes for the day. It wasn't until a couple of weeks later that I found out he was an ex-cop. Still wary of authority and the old 'enemy', I might have had a problem with this if I'd have known from the start, but he had become a friend by then.

Suddenly I was a student, sitting at a desk for the first time in years, trying to study church history, hermeneutics, Greek and loads of other stuff I knew nothing about. I couldn't even speak English properly, let alone Greek! And why did I need to know about things that had happened hundreds of years ago? I love history now, but back then it was so boring.

I also found being obedient to tutors and the system incredibly hard. I had been used to telling my gang what to do, and they would do anything I wanted. Now *I* was being told what to do. I was one of the oldest students and didn't have a long concentration span, so being forced to listen to all this stuff felt really alien to me.

However, it was also an incredible experience. I would often look at myself in the classroom window close to my desk and wonder: 'Is that really me?' It was so unreal, considering what my life had been like, but also a great privilege. As I started to get my head round it all, I found out that I actually had a brain and loved to study. I had a great respect for our tutors and loved to listen to them talking about something that they really knew inside out. I was learning so much and was hungry for more. Even in my free time and during lunchtimes, I would go and see the chef and he would let me use a quiet room near the kitchens to sit and study in.

We started to put our learning into practice by going out on the streets. The first time it happened we were in Salisbury handing out leaflets containing information about God. Some young kids were pushing my arm away as I tried to hand them out. I felt my temper rising, but God stopped me doing anything more and none of them got battered!

In my second year, I wanted to attend a well-known free pop festival at Stonehenge, in Salisbury, to tell everyone there about God. I managed to persuade a few other college students to go with me, but on the way I ended up crashing into the back of a lorry. I had tried to overtake it on a straight bit of road, but the lorry driver had to slam his brakes on when the car in front of him suddenly turned left. This sent the lorry's rear end crashing through my windscreen, ending up about two inches from my face. We'd just picked up a hitchhiker, who decided to go and get a safer ride somewhere else! In fact, when this happened, I said to him: 'I'm a Christian and all sorts of strange things happen when you are a Christian!' How right I was.

We had to return to college and I set off again on another day but this time I was on my own. It was an illegal pop festival, surrounded by police with a helicopter hovering over the site. I bounced over the rough makeshift driveway into the field, parked up and started talking to people. Looking around I could follow the main drag as it swept in a loop around the site. Between two lorries, I spotted a camp fire with some people milling around, so I made my way towards them. It turned out to be a group of my old Hell's Angel mates from Leigh Park. I had to talk to them, but I asked permission of the leader, who used to be my old vice president. I gave them a few leaflets. While I stood with one of them, we watched another guy we both knew well swaggering past.

'Was I ever as bad as him?' I asked.

'No, Brian. You were ten times worse.'

Not everyone was keen to speak to me though. I tried talking to one guy and quickly realised that he didn't want to know.

'Clear off, will you? On yer bike,' he said angrily, glaring at me.

When I tried to hand him a leaflet, he said: 'Tell you what. If I promise you I will read it, will you clear off and leave me alone?'

I agreed. He'd given me his word.

Years later, when my first book was released, I was doing some promotional work at Spring Harvest, a well-known Christian holiday event. When the crowds had gone and things had quietened down, someone approached me who I didn't recognise.

'Remember years ago at that Stonehenge pop festival, you handed me a tract?' he said. 'I promised to read it to make you go away and I did. Because of that, I'm a Christian now.' He was working for a Christian publishing company attending the event and was involved in selling my book.

I love to hear stories like that. It's incredibly encouraging and thrills my heart to lead someone to the Lord, even when I'm drained, dog-tired and having a tough time. It still blows me away to be used by God like this.

But I was never far from trouble! Leaving the pop festival, I was stopped by the police, who took my details and ended up prosecuting me for trespassing. Oddly enough there had been loads of police around the gate when I went in and none of them warned me that I was about to trespass.

My church weren't impressed. It wasn't the 'done thing' apparently for a Christian to end up in court. But how come they supported someone who broke the law as a 'God smuggler', sneaking Bibles illegally into communist countries? Surely that was the same, wasn't it, helping someone by being unlawful? There was a lot about Christianity and the Church that I found very confusing and contradictory. It still really grieves me that Christians can be so damaging and so unaware of the effect of what they are saying. At the time I just focused on soaking up more of God to try and get my head round it all.

I remember offending two old ladies the first time I preached in a church. I was far from eloquent and gifted in speaking well, but I preached my guts out. The following week one of my tutors, a very sensitive and lovely man, called me into his office. He had been listening to my sermon that day.

'Do you know that you said "damn" twice when you were speaking in church?' I just looked at him with a blank face. What was so bad about that? He told me that two old ladies in the congregation were shuddering, they were so shocked at this language. Back then, in the mid 1970s, it was considered to be a very impolite word, but I had no idea that I would be giving offence. My language was more street than church.

One day, an Irish lad, John from our Bible college invited me to go with him on a week-long mission to Northern Ireland. This was at the height of the major troubles between Catholics and Protestants in the mid-1970s and we were going to some of the worst-hit areas like the Falls Road, the main road through west Belfast where a lot of conflict took place.

Arriving there, we started out in Crossmaglen, County Armagh, which had a bustling open-air market. To one side stood a police station with metal-plated reinforced walls and covered in barbed wire. Police helicopters were regularly coming in to land. There I visited the offices of Sinn Fein, the republican party associated with the provisional IRA. I wanted to win them for the Lord and pretty soon they put out a description in their newssheet of an SAS sergeant, big built and long-haired, going round pretending to be a civilian. It felt like they were talking about me.

I knew I was at risk then. Out on the green a Landrover appeared and John told me it was an IRA commander. He was staring at us, watching our every move. Over on the other side of the green were a couple of old guys. One of them looked vaguely familiar. John saw me looking. 'Do you know a guy called Bobby Smith?' he said.

'Yeah, I was in Chelmsford with him.'

'Well, that's him over there.' I couldn't believe it was him and realised he would have been looking at me in exactly the same way. I quickly rolled up my sleeves and showed my tattoos. He came over. 'Are you Brian Greenaway?'

'Yeah. Are you Bobby Smith?'

'Yeah.' Nothing more was said and he swaggered off. Pretty soon he disappeared. But the result was that the IRA commander then realised that I wasn't a threat and not part of the SAS, because Bobby had been talking to me and had clearly told them who I really was.

John told me that there was a woman living down a nearby road who knew me and wanted to meet me. I had no idea who she was. It was dark by now. As we started walking towards the road where she lived, we saw that all the streetlights were off.

'Someone is about to get shot,' John explained. We walked nervously down the road, me pretending to whistle to give the impression that I wasn't scared, like I did as a youngster travelling home on dark country roads. Suddenly a woman came flying out of a house and grabbed me, crying: 'Brian!' It was someone I had known from Leigh Park days.

She invited us in. On the wall was an Irish flag and a list of IRA martyrs killed in the conflict. A couple of young lads, aged about nineteen or twenty, were standing nearby. I was told they were bombers. They treated me like I was a hero and I used the opportunity to tell them my story.

We had planned to go to a youth club on the Falls Road, but couldn't find it. We ended up driving up and down looking for it. John told me that there would now be guns pointed at us, because you never ride up and down the Falls Road, you go up and out as quickly as possible. I later made a phone call and while I was talking, my friend was being interrogated outside by a group of guys because there was a Brit with him.

Often while driving we spotted the tops of heads in ditches. British soldiers were everywhere, watching for trouble. I went over to one patrol once and asked one of them where he was from, suddenly realising my mistake. You don't ask these men any questions and here was I asking them where they were from. I told him I was a Christian on a mission. He was shocked.

'You've got some bottle. I'm only here because I've got to be here.'

Danger was everywhere. We walked past a small church that had been all over the news when it was machine-gunned while the congregation were inside. Another time we heard strange noises from a barn near one of the province borders. It sounded like someone who was getting a real thrashing.

'What's that?' I asked John.

'Don't ask,' he said. 'Let's get out of here quickly.'

This was a challenging week, but we really saw God's hand on us. He kept us safe and it was like He had planned the chance meeting with Bobby, who I hadn't seen for years, to happen just at the right time when I needed it.

Back at college, I managed to get through the two years, often slowly and painfully. Near the end of my second year I was desperate to get someone to tell my old mates on Leigh Park about Jesus. I couldn't think of a single time that someone had told me when I was part of that scene. I also felt bad that I had led a lot of them into drugs and violence and now some of them were dead. I felt partly to blame. I wanted to give something back to that community.

At college we had a lot of visits from evangelists who spoke about their work, and I often asked them if they had ever considered going to Leigh Park. One had been but vowed never to go again after his tent ropes had been cut and he'd been given a lot of grief. The others weren't interested. I felt very angry about this because I had a real passion for the people of that area.

I was telling one of the visiting lecturers all this, when he suddenly said to me, 'Why don't you go?' Of course, why didn't I think of that? Then again I knew nothing about running a mission and I still had plenty of enemies there.

I travelled back to Leigh Park to talk to one of the ministers about my ideas. He offered the use of his church next to a pub that I used to hang around in. How come I'd never noticed this church before? How blind I had been!

While I was there I met up with my mate Steve and took him for a pub lunch. I told him all about Jesus and as a result, my dear friend asked Jesus into his life. He really wanted to be forgiven for the bad things that he had done and to see God working in his life. Sadly his commitment to his faith wasn't to last, as I found out many years later.

The ten-day mission was a real success. Assisted by a team of other college students, we leafleted the estate and had a packed church every night. We performed sketches, had gospel bands, testimonies and a showing of the film version of the Nicky Cruz story *Run Baby Run*. I talked every night about what God had done in my life. So many people were moved by the stories and eighteen became Christians. We prayed with them and linked them with local churches.

I learned a lot here about myself, but not all of it was good. I still wrestled with my humanity and it was so easy for me to get things wrong. One evening I was going into a pub with my mates and a guy approached me. 'You're Brian Greenaway,' he said. 'Can I have a word?'

'No, I'm with my mates,' I told him. I later realised that I'd missed an opportunity to share something about God.

At the end of my second year at college, I received my two-year diploma. I had no idea where God wanted me to be, so I decided that until I had some clear direction, I would stay on at college. One day into the third year, we had a visiting speaker who wore a nice suit and carried a large Bible. As I listened to him talk about his work in the London City Mission, I thought, who wants to go to London to work? I had visited previously and remembered walking along Bond Street chewing grit and dust. Give me the country any day; no way would I go to London! Later the minister at the church I attended, a man very much on fire for God, told me that he had been in the LCM and he had enjoyed it. And then suddenly I found myself being sent on a two-week placement, to the London City Mission of all places! This had to be a joke. Despite all my protests and rebellion, there was no getting away from it.

Heading over to Hoxton on my first day, I thought I would easily get there in half an hour. But it took me half an hour just to cross Tower Bridge. How on earth do people cope with London life? I was soon taught how to run a mission hall and how to reach out to people in need. The following week I got up very early to attend the flower market with an LCM worker and chat to the flower sellers. This was nothing like I had thought it would be. Thinking back to the LCM speaker at college, I thought I would have to carry a big Bible and go door-knocking. That was nowhere near where I was at – not in a million years. Give me pop festivals any day, where I can merge and fit in.

There was one situation that nearly pushed me over the edge. We were expected to stand on a soap box in Tower Hill to preach to the public. We had loads of gay guys gathering round, ribbing us. I'd had enough.

'If you don't shut up I'm going to rip your throat out,' I yelled. Back at HQ I was immediately called to the boss's office.

'Look,' I told him, 'I'm no good at street preaching and if they have a pop at me, I'll have a pop back. Don't put me in a place where I'm tempted to blow.'

Returning to college, I had a strong sense that God wanted me to work in the LCM. The dilemma was that I loved the country and longed for a home close to the sea in a quiet location. London just wasn't me. But I needed to be obedient and applied anyway, even though I kept trying to sabotage the process! In interview after interview I made it very clear that I didn't want to work in London, even though I felt that perhaps God was calling me to do so. But I was still given a job and undertook two months' training in South Ealing. In some ways it did my head in because I had to study basic stuff again, when I'd already covered the subjects in-depth at college.

During this time I visited a lot of old, lonely people, many of them too proud to admit that they were lonely. There were many sad situations. I used to play darts with one old man and persuaded him to start attending a men's meeting. Sometime later he missed a visit. I went to see him that day and found out he'd been unwell and passing blood. The hospital hadn't helped.

'Why did they send you home?' I asked him.

'They said they couldn't do anything for me.' He died the next morning.

Despite the pain and the difficulties, I knew this was what I wanted to do; reach out and help real people.

However, I told God and the LCM that I would only work in London under certain conditions. I didn't want to work under anyone else and I wanted my own mission hall. This was unheard of for a new recruit, but there was no way I could do anything else. I got what I asked for, but it was in one of the roughest areas in London, the Isle of Dogs. This two-mile stretch of deserted and run-down dockland is tucked in a U-bend on the River Thames. It was a nightmarish, horrific, tough place full of council houses, unemployment, violence and crime. I took a visiting friend on a tour one evening, encountered a violent racial row between two neighbours and later heard of a guy having his fingers cut off for refusing to sell cigarettes to a minor.

My new mission hall had thieves scaling the walls at night carrying stolen goods home and my car, my pride and joy, vanished overnight. It was a Cortina with an old American rebel flag painted on it. People got to know me and my car very quickly. I spent hours one day fitting a new gearbox, under the watchful eye of local villains hanging around on a nearby corner. The next morning I went out to take it for a ride and check out the engine. It wasn't there! I was gobsmacked. Who had the right to nick my car? I'd seen youngsters joyriding stolen cars around the local mud shoot, often with kids clinging to the roofs, risking their lives. They usually wrecked them or set fire to them and disappeared. I suspect my car went for a swim in the local docks.

One of my jobs was helping to run a local youth club, where I was regularly threatened with violence. But most of my work involved knocking on doors and trying to talk to people about God. Many times the door would be shut in my face or I would face abuse. Sometimes when I handed out leaflets, a few minutes later the door would open and they would be thrown in the outside bin. I know that not everyone wants to know about Jesus and I had to keep reminding myself that I would have been the same at one time. But it seemed that nobody wanted to know. It was incredibly tough. Added to that was the constant financial struggle of trying to survive on a wage that was so low that I was able to claim free milk and bread for the family I had by then. When it all got too much, which was quite often, I used to escape into one of the quieter parks on the island to sit and cry, praying for strength. Another source of comfort came from visiting some of the older Christians in the district. Instead of being abused on doorsteps, I was made welcome and we read the Bible together, talked about the problems in the area and prayed. It gave me a lot of strength. I also met with local ministers and Christian workers once a month to talk things over and pray together.

I always did what I could to help those in need. I remember one dear old man, Fred, who was a retired foreman in the local docks, back in the days when all foremen wore bowler hats. I visited him regularly and saw his health deteriorate. I never saw his family visit him, but I spoke to them and they told me that he needed to be in a home. He refused to go.

He was incontinent and I would often help to clean him up and take his trousers home to wash them for him. But when he started collapsing, I worried that he wouldn't be able to get up again. A couple of times he collapsed close to the electric fire and got burned. In the end I managed to persuade him to go into a home and found him a place in a Christian-run home about fifty miles away. He was able to take a little of his own furniture and I helped him settle in. He was made very welcome.

Good things like this did happen on the island, but they were rare. It was an incredibly difficult four years and most days I felt like I was banging my head against a brick wall. But God was toughening me up in a different way, using the man that I was, to turn me into the man that I am now. It helped to prepare me for what was about to happen next.

— CHAPTER 9 —

What's so special about me?

One day I was contacted by Lion Publishing to ask if I was interested in writing a book about my life. I was at a loss to know how they had heard of me, but I soon discovered that one of the ministers from our monthly meetings had written to them about me. He had already had a book published with them. I was a bit bewildered by their interest. Why on earth would they want to write a book about me? Who am I, really? I'm just a bad guy that became a Christian, like so many others. But it was a book that had helped bring me to Christ. What if my story could do the same for others? I decided to go ahead with it.

Going through the process of working on the book, I still wasn't sure if it would be any good or whether people would want to read it. I didn't know whether it was exciting or dramatic enough. But at the end of the day, even though we had to water down some of the graphic descriptions of what I had done, it was real. It happened. It was me, warts and all.

In 1982 *Hell's Angel* was published. It quickly became a bestseller, was translated into many languages (it was the first English Christian paperback to go into Greece) and sold all over the world. Suddenly I was thrust into the limelight and into a lifestyle that was totally alien to me. I was interviewed on radio and television, asked to speak to crowds of thousands in big arenas and football grounds, invited to the Houses of Parliament and many well-known private schools and met prestigious individuals and groups that I would never normally have mixed with. It was exciting, humbling and a tremendous privilege, but at times it was also confusing, uncomfortable and frustrating.

I used to wonder why people assumed that because I'd written a book, I could suddenly give eloquent interviews and speeches to large audiences. How did they know I could even do joined-up speaking? For all they knew, I could have stood up in front of all their invited and important guests and said something like: 'Er ... hell ... er ... hello ... I ... I ... I'm B-B-B-B-Brian G-G-G-Greenaway ... and ... er ... and ... er ... I w-w-w-wanted to t-t-talk ... er ... to you ...'

I didn't do that! But I do know that God took what I said in so many of these situations and used it to reach people. I remember speaking at a house group in Maidstone and the leaders said to everyone present: 'This is the guy who is going to change your life.'

'You're joking, aren't you?' I said, gobsmacked. But several of those present who were non-Christians committed their lives to Christ that night. Once more God took me by surprise.

Once I was invited to the Lord Mayor's banqueting house in London. I was the after-dinner speaker at the Livery Lounge Party, and during dinner sat next to the top Mason in England. As I was speaking I was aware that he was very moved by what I was saying. Afterwards he said to me, 'Brian, we have had all sorts of speakers here and you have moved me like I just can't believe with your story.'

Later I was shown a list of previous speakers and I couldn't believe that I had followed in these men's footsteps. Men such as – Lord Longford, labour peer and campaigner for penal reform– Sir Francis Chichester, aviator and the first person to sail round the world single-handedly – T.S. Eliot – Lord Hunt, who climbed Everest – Bishop David Sheppard – Lord

Wakeham, the Press Complaints' Board – Sir Alec Rose, who also sailed around the world single-handedly and Luis Palau, well-known international evangelist ... and then there was me, Brian Greenaway! It was mind-blowing.

What was also mind-blowing in places like this, was working out which cutlery to use! I was a rough country guy, a former Hell's Angel, an ex-con. I didn't have a clue how to eat in polite society. I mean, which one of the endless rows of knives and forks do I start with? How am I supposed to eat corn on a cob? Do I slice it off or just start chewing it? How about a leg of chicken? I usually just pick it up and bite it, but was that acceptable? I felt very self-conscious and awkward.

The friend who invited me to the mayoral event whispered in my ear at dinner, 'Whatever you do, pass the port to the left when it goes round. And don't guzzle it from the bottle.' As if I would. I don't even like port!

At times my reputation went before me, like the time I preached to the Coldstream Guards in Westminster. The lieutenant colonel invited me to speak at their chapel in Birdcage Walk, and when I arrived, the armed soldier at the entrance knew who I was straightaway.

'You're Brian Greenaway, aren't you?' he said.

'Yeah, how did you know?'

'This is a one-way street and you have just come up the wrong way.' Only I could do that!

The Coldstream Guards is the oldest regiment of the British army, mainly responsible for ceremonial and royal duties. Their chapel was lined with old flags that had been shot to pieces. At the end was a huge, high pulpit that I was expected to climb up into, and filling the seats were crowds of men waiting to hear me speak.

'How do I talk to people like you?' I told them. 'All I know is that you are men and I love to talk to men. But I have to say that some of you lot are better tooled up than I used to be in my days with the Angels, with all your machine guns and flipping swords!'

It was a very special time and I was invited back to speak to them again.

They were all in a different league from me, though. On two occasions, I was invited to speak at the prestigious Stowe School, Buckingham. I preached in their church about how certain things blew me away, like mathematics. I used an example of a sphere and described its size.

'How many square inches is that?' I asked. I had no idea how you would work that out. 'I've no idea. I'm not clever like you lot!' I said and carried on. (I often have a crack at the audience and if someone comes in late, I'll say to them: 'Where have you been, then?')

I noticed a lad with his head down working on something so, of course, I picked on him! 'Hey, you, what are you doing?'

He said: 'I'm just working it out for you.' And he told me the answer!

There were times when mixing with such awfully nice people was great fun, especially getting behind the wheel of a Rolls for the first time. I preached at a posh church near Guildford and a wealthy businessman from the congregation took me home for dinner afterwards. He let me drive his car and as soon as I climbed in the driver's seat and put my foot down, it shot off at great speed. It was a two-and-a-half ton car that responded like you wouldn't believe. We arrived at his house and when he opened the door, I realised that it wasn't a house. It was a large garage, full of vintage cars. Some years later he was generous enough to buy me a Corsa 1100cc which, at my size, I had to cram myself into. He was a lovely and special Christian man.

But sometimes I felt like people treated me as if I was public property and took liberties. They would take pictures of me and film me without asking. I was fuming once at Manchester

Central Hall when someone filmed me without asking permission or explaining what it was for. And at times not even the five-star hotels offered any comfort. I remember being in one in Liverpool and when I shut the door, it didn't feel like a hotel room, it suddenly felt like a prison cell. I felt trapped.

Another thing I hated was being hero-worshipped because I really didn't deserve it. I had a phone call once from this over-excited woman: 'Is that Brian Greenaway?' she said.

'Yes.'

'Is that really Brian Greenaway?'

'Yeah, this is really Brian Greenaway.' She was acting like she was talking to someone famous like Cliff Richard, I mean, come on get a life! But it all I'm totally intolerant of it. It doesn't embarrass me – it frustrates me. I believe that anyone's testimony is as powerful as mine because of what God has done for us. And I know who I am, saved by God's grace.

The publicity stuff went on for some years and often the scale of it was mind-blowing. On one world service radio station for the British forces I found out that 400 million people were listening. Once when I spoke at Queen's Park Rangers football stadium alongside Luis Palau, I cracked a joke and it took ages for the laughter to ripple round the thousands of people sat listening in this huge place. I just couldn't get my head round things like that. It was unreal.

But the real reason I wrote the book was to show people how God can change lives, and I'm both amazed and humbled at just how many people have come to Christ through reading it. I remember being in Westminster and meeting the chairman of the Conservative Christian Association. He told me that he became a Christian because of reading my book. Even now, twenty years later, I still get contacted by people telling me how much the book spoke to them and how God changed their lives because of it. That makes me feel fantastic.

What really changed the direction of my life was when my book started going into prisons. Suddenly I was receiving hundreds of letters from prisoners and I wanted to respond to every one. Sometimes I had up to 250 letters to reply to, which was all done by hand. There were no computers back then.

I also received invitations to visit prisons in both the UK and abroad. I had visited one prison since finishing my last sentence. At Bible college I went with a team into Feltham Young Offenders' Institution, south west London, to give my testimony. I was told by officers that I could say what I wanted as long as I didn't talk about prison. That was like gagging me, but God was in it so powerfully because I did what they asked. I could have easily said: 'On your bike, I'm an ex-con. I'll do what I want!' That would not have been what God wanted from me.

This time I wasn't so restricted and ended up giving talks all over the country. But eventually it felt wrong for me to be a London City Missionary when I wasn't spending much time in London. I talked to my boss about it and he had been thinking the same thing.

Resigning was a risk because it would mean having no job and no income, but I knew that God was leading me in a new direction and my life was about to change again. It was time to step out in faith.

— CHAPTER 10 —

Back behind bars

When God started leading me towards prison work, I moved to Wandsworth and set up the Brian Greenaway Trust. This eventually became The 25 Trust, based on the words of Jesus in Matthew:

> 'For I was hungry and you gave me something to eat, I was thirsty and you gave me something to drink, I was a stranger and you invited me in, I needed clothes and you clothed me, I was sick and you looked after me, I was in prison and you came to visit me ... I tell you the truth, whatever you did for one of the least of these brothers of mine, you did for me.' (Matthew 25:35–36,40)

'The 25 Trust' was much better because the 'Brian Greenaway Trust' meant that the focus was on Brian Greenaway, who is a rather sad character, let's face it! But it's not about him – Brian Greenaway. It's about Him – God.

I had the support of a number of godly Christian men who became my trustees. They don't tell me what to do; they are there to encourage and help me in my ministry. Some have moved on after various disagreements, but others have stayed with me for a long time. My chairman, John Field, has now been with me for twenty-eight years.

We relied on our church and other Christian supporters for funding. I've had some brilliant supporters over the years, but it was often a financial struggle. God always provided though, and I even managed to get a mortgage, despite not having a guaranteed income. A friend of mine who owned a light aeroplane, which he took me out in regularly, said he knew someone who could guarantee a mortgage for me. I filled out the papers and he sent them off. However, when I had a call from the mortgage company, I realised he'd lied on the form. I told them that certain things written weren't true. They said they respected my honesty and decided to grant me the mortgage anyway, when I really should have been refused one. It seemed like God was honouring the truth.

As an ex-con, visiting prisons in those early days often meant that prison officers and other staff were suspicious of me, but over time they got used to me and some were very supportive. For example, when I visited Strangeways in Manchester, invited by chaplain Noel Proctor who had moved there from Dartmoor, my car was broken into the night before. I had been speaking at a huge hall on the Saturday evening and when we came out, someone had smashed a window of our car and stolen our bags. The next morning I was at Strangeways. When I told staff my car had no window, they allowed me to take my car into the prison. In the church service there were two exits for the prisoners and at the end of the service, the senior officer on duty told the staff to shut one door, so instead of the prisoners being herded out quickly, they all got to speak to me.

Another officer helped to find a cool place for the two German Shepherds I owned at the time to keep them out of the sun. This was at Camp Hill Prison, one of three prisons on the Isle of Wight (now amalgamated with Albany and Parkhurst Prison and called HMP Isle of Wight), where I visited regularly. It wasn't an easy place to get to because I had to catch an early morning ferry from Portsmouth. I can understand why lads don't like being sent to the island because it makes it hard for family and friends to visit them.

I had given the dogs a walk and now needed to find a place to park that was out of the sun and under the trees. Suddenly the main gate opened and a dog handler came out.

'I've been watching you on the security cameras. Why not park over there?' he suggested, pointing under some trees.

'Is that OK?' I asked. This was an area where parking isn't permitted.

'Sure, no problem.' It was a blessing to find another dog lover at a time of need.

I found another one in Parkhurst, the high security prison on the island. I started talking to this dog handler outside the chapel, I was admiring his sniffer dog and he asked if I would like to see his dog working. After talking to the prisoners, I went to watch in the kennels and training area behind the chapel, where he had lined up some chairs with items of clothing on. Some had drugs in them and the dog had to locate the drugs, which he did easily. They were a great team and it felt like a privilege to be treated in this way.

There were times when even the staff were touched by God, and one of these was in Parkhurst. I had been talking to the lads in the chapel about sin, explaining that we all sin and Jesus didn't come for those who considered themselves to be good. I later found out that one of the officers standing at the back really felt the message was for him and he later became a Christian and ended up training to become a church minister.

Another prison I worked in regularly was Winchester, where I visited three times a month to take Sunday services and midweek meetings in the chapel. I was able to develop good, working relationships with both prisoners and some staff.

A lot of this work I did alone, but in some prisons I was joined at Sunday services by a team of young, keen Christians from Warlingham, Surrey, who would sing and perform sketches.

This was always enjoyed by the prisoners. The team were very dedicated to the work and would come out in all weathers. I was so proud of them all for their commitment. I remember one Sunday when they met up with me in a freezing blizzard on a main road near to Warlingham. As we travelled together, Karen, the team organiser drove behind me and as we hit the roundabout, I saw in the rear-view mirror that she skidded on the ice. Her car spun a full 360 degrees and she just drove on!

But accidents do happen, especially when you are doing a lot of travelling. Once when we were down at Dover Prison (now Dover Immigration Removal Centre), which we visited regularly, one of the team members drove into the back of me as we went through the prison gate. She apologised, looking really worried, as if I was about to attack her! I told her not to worry. It was just a little bump.

Despite any problems, it was worth all the effort to take the gospel to guys who often believed they were too bad to be loved by God. I was usually given the freedom to tell my story and share the Bible with prisoners, even though I wasn't permitted to make 'altar calls', asking them to stand up or come to the front if they wanted to become Christians. We didn't want to put the spotlight on anyone who responded. But many guys listened to what I said and wanted God in their lives. I was able to keep in touch with a large number of them for some years after their release.

Not all of them came to the chapel to hear about God, though. Some just wanted a chance to get out of their cell. Others were genuinely curious about me and wanted to check me out. Some would meet up with their co-de (co-defendant) from another wing to plan their court appearances and make sure their stories matched up. It was also a place where drug dealers would meet and do deals. One such prisoner was a London guy called Jake. He had been a driver for a heavy firm and had got banged up in Wandsworth for driving into a police officer, dragging him several hundred yards up the road.

As Jake sat in the chapel listening to me speaking about God's love for us all, he started getting angry. More than anything he wanted to attack me, but because he had drugs on him he couldn't do anything. If he did, he'd be taken to the block, searched and busted for possession.

That night in prison he couldn't sleep. He kept hearing my voice in his head repeatedly saying: 'Jesus loves you'. Eventually dawn broke. Restless and exhausted, he got up, knelt by his bed and prayed: 'Jesus, if You are really there, come into my life and forgive me.' What happened next blew him away. He felt that Jesus really came into the cell with him. He had no doubt at all that God was in his life and he started to change.

We met up several times after his release, when he moved into the country to escape his old friends, who were afraid that now he was a Christian he would grass them up. However, it wasn't easy for him. I don't think his wife was in the least bit interested in his new-found faith. In fact, she called their black cat Satan and he had to stand at the doorstep every night shouting: 'Satan, come in.' He was finding it hard to travel anywhere without a car, so I gave him my Rover SDI. That's God's economy – people give to me in times of need and I give to others. He went on to lead a number of others to Christ, even though he felt his life was in danger from his old friends.

Being a Christian in prison is hard, as I found out, but it can be even more difficult on release. Guys often return to their home area where there are so many temptations to mix with old mates and drift back into criminal activities. They are known to police, so their cards are marked and they will be watched, questioned and searched. Not long after being released from one of my prison sentences, I remember being stopped and searched three times in one day!

I saw many men come to Christ in prison and very few people on the out, it seemed, were prepared to help them. There were some Christian organisations for ex-offenders, but they had such rigid restrictions around who they would and would not help, I just got fed up with it all. But it really played on my mind.

I talked over my worries with a prayer group that I met regularly with near Wandsworth prison. As a result the Stepping Stones Trust was born to provide halfway houses for these men. The Trust continues to thrive and now has three homes for Christian ex-offenders in London, supported by local churches. The Trust is a real blessing and support to guys when they come out of prison, in much the same way that the Coke Hole Trust helped me. I remained a founder trustee for some time, but my day-to-day involvement with the Trust was short-lived. I didn't want to burn up my energies on other external commitments when I'd been called to work with prisoners. I wasn't Superman and could only do so much.

However, before I focused fully on prison work, it seemed that God had another job for me. One freezing cold winter evening I was watching television, feeling snug and warm, when a programme came on about the homeless in London. I saw people lying in the streets – cold, alone and covered in snow. Nobody cared about them and nobody missed them. It stirred up painful memories of what that was like when I left home as a teenager. I couldn't get these images out of my mind. I needed to do something.

In the end I phoned a mate. Not quite sure what we could do, we decided to start going out with food and hot drinks around Waterloo station, the Strand and Lincoln's Inn Fields – the largest public square in London. As the work built up, we got hold of a large bus to take out food and the Salvation Army shop in Wandsworth donated clothes. We ended up with a team of ten volunteers, mostly Christians. The only rule I insisted on was that we asked no questions. Homeless people are suspicious of everyone. But it's actually very hard to have a conversation with someone when you can't ask anything.

I will never, ever forget how cold it was on the streets that winter. We needed something more to offer them.

One day, a lady contacted me to say that there was an old, empty children's hospital near the Elephant and Castle and the owner had given permission for it to be used as a night shelter for homeless people. What a brilliant answer to prayer. This was just what we needed. Slowly we worked the streets and encouraged people into the shelter, once they had overcome their suspicions. Some medical volunteers joined us, the army gave us a field kitchen and more people helped out or donated goods. One evening, a well-known actor arrived secretly with a huge pile of blankets for us. He hadn't done it in public just so that people would think he was a good guy, it was a genuine act of compassion.

Over the months we got to know the homeless guys well. Some told us they had been in the army and fought in the Falklands. Others told us stories of family rejection. For some, drink had a bad hold on them. We just listened. We weren't there to judge.

But we knew God was working among them. One evening a big guy came over to us in tears, hunched over, with his hands under his armpits. He was freezing cold. I was driving a big Shogun by then and I helped him climb into my motor. He was so cold, he could hardly move. I put my arm around him and said: 'Look, I don't normally do this, but can I pray for you?'

'Yes, please,' he sobbed. I asked God to reach out to him. There was little else I could do. As I was praying, he started feeling so warm, that he took his jacket off. We were able to find him a bed for the night in a nearby shelter.

Another time I met a really smart, clean and tidy guy on the streets who didn't look like any of the other homeless people. Despite the 'no questions' rule, I had to find out why he was different. He told me that his business had folded up and suddenly, overnight, he had lost everything. My heart went out to him and I promised myself that I would keep an eye on him. The following week he had disappeared.

'How come, guys? What's happened to him?' I asked the other homeless people. They explained that his mates had come looking for him and taken him home with them. I think he had been too proud to ask for help, but they found him.

We managed to help a lot of people, but we couldn't save everyone. Once the police found a dead body in our hostel. We believe it was one of the homeless guys that had died in his sleep. Others simply couldn't survive on the streets. One of these was Bridget. She would usually be drunk by the time we arrived at Lincoln's Inn Fields and she always made a beeline for me to give me a cuddle. One of our girls would take her away and talk with her. We found out that Bridget was being beaten and abused by some of the homeless guys. We didn't find out who did it because we didn't ask questions, but one week we arrived and Bridget wasn't around. We later found out that she had died from the cold. That same week there was a documentary on TV about the homeless in London which I believe included something of Bridget. The show was aptly called *Dying for a Home*.

Not everyone was grateful for our support, though. We were often threatened. At first it was almost like a rite of passage, testing us out to see how we responded. But I wasn't going to take it lying down. Once we saw a load of men walking round with big lumps of wood, looking like they were ready to attack. Another time, down in Waterloo handing out food and blankets, a guy swaggered over.

'Are you Christians?' he asked.

'Yes,' I said, smiling at him.

'We overturn Christian vans down here,' he threatened, smiling back.

'Well, I'll bet with you now that this is one van you don't turn over, mate,' I replied calmly, still smiling.

'If you want to play, I'll play with you.' He walked away.

I don't think they would have respected us if we'd have fallen over from fright as soon as they said: 'Boo!' I knew that I wasn't called by God to be a doormat or cowpat to be trodden all over. I wasn't going to lie down and take it if they tried to give me a kicking. I was prepared to defend myself and my team. But however hard it got, we were determined to be there for them.

There was only one night when there was any real trouble. Someone came looking for me and I realised it was Carl, a lad that I had been writing to when he had been in prison. He told me how he had nicked a motor when he got out, so he could come up to London and see me. We gave him a hot drink and had a chat. Suddenly another guy appeared.

'Are you Christians?' he asked.

'Most of us are,' I told him.

'This is what I think of Christians,' he said, as he grabbed Carl's hot drink and threw it over him.

'You shouldn't have done that,' I said. Carl flipped, punching him to the ground and then giving him one hell of a kicking. I told my team to get in the van and warned Carl that he had better split. We needed to call an ambulance and it was better if he wasn't on the scene.

Some of the team wanted to get out of the van and help the badly injured guy, but I wouldn't let them. There were concerns over catching AIDS by this time and I wouldn't allow them to touch someone who was bleeding.

It was a very telling experience. It felt like God had shown me in a quick and bad way who I used to be and how I used to behave. I would have reacted in exactly the same way.

After a while I started to get a bit fed up with the attitude of some of those we were trying to help. When I had been hungry,

I was never fussy about what I ate. Now we had guys getting stroppy with us for all manner of silly things. So one evening as we were pulling out to go into London, I told my team that when we arrived, they were to stay in the van until I had spoken to the people who would be waiting for us. I was going to read them the riot act. I was a bit surprised when we arrived that there was a very big crowd of guys. I got out of the van and had a go at the waiting crowd. I told them that it never hurt to say thank you when we gave them something, and to moan about the food was out of order. We had worked hard for some time preparing to bring it out.

'We are here for the homeless, so if you don't need anything, then leave us alone,' I shouted at them. Looking around they seemed to be stunned into silence.

Suddenly I heard someone in the crowd say, 'Yeah, well done Brian.' It ended up being the best and politest evening we ever had with them.

While doing the homeless work I was still out visiting prisons and writing to a lot of men inside, who I had either met and wanted to continue supporting, or who had read my book. Sometimes, even to this day, I come across guys that I wrote to or saw in the past – sometimes twenty years ago – and they still remember me. That means a lot and I find it really encouraging.

But while the ministry was going well and I was seeing God touch so many lives, my personal life was gradually falling apart. I was about to face one of the darkest and most devastating periods of my life.

CHAPTER II

Never will I leave you

While I was at Moorlands Bible College, I met a girl, fell in love, got married and had a family. But gradually, over the years, things started to go wrong. I don't want to go into the details of what happened in order to protect my children and their privacy (which is also why I haven't mentioned them in this book), but the result was that the marriage collapsed and we ended up getting divorced.

When my marriage fell apart, so did I. For the next thirteen months of my life, I was in pieces. I cried constantly. I wouldn't answer the door or the phone. I was absolutely slashed apart, mentally devastated and in total depression. And I was so angry with God that I had to go through it all. I couldn't believe that my life had ended up like this. It was worse than the lowest points I had ever previously had, even the times when I didn't have God in my life.

What made it worse was that I was well known as a full-time Christian worker, the Rev Brian Greenaway, with a bestselling book and many high-profile public appearances. And now I was getting divorced. I was judged and rejected by nearly all of my so-called Christian friends who didn't know the details of what had happened.

There were a few genuine ones who stood by me. One of them was Mark Birchall, one of my trustees. He was a very busy and in-demand city gent, who worked hard to earn his wealth, retired early and threw himself into Christian work. I remember going to see him, throwing my arms around him, hugging him and crying. He told me: 'Brian, I can't possibly understand what you are going through; I've never been in this situation, but I'm here with you and I'm standing with you.'

Years later, when he was suffering from terminal cancer, I visited him on the afternoon before he died. He was in a coma, but I held his hand and with tears pouring down my face I said: 'Mark, do you remember what you did for me and how you supported me when I went through everything? Thank you so much for being there for me.' Mark was a real Christian man.

Most of the others turned their backs on me. Up until that point, so many had wanted to be my friend. I had loads of friends when I was on a high and in the spotlight, being chauffeur driven and speaking in awfully nice places where everyone is clapping, cheering, treating me like a hero and saying: 'Oh, isn't Brian wonderful?' But what about when I'm lying in the gutter in agony, bruised, battered, spitting blood and crying my guts out? Where were my 'friends' then? In truth, I felt alone. Totally alone.

It seems that some people in the Church think that when a Christian gets it wrong, he has failed completely and that's it, game over. Surely the Bible tells us that all of us get it wrong and let God down, and that none of us is perfect. We are saved by grace and not by works. Yet we can be so quick to judge others. During my years as a Christian, I have met so many people who have been rejected by those in the Church who have pointed out their failings. We've met so many Christians who have been thrown out of church because they got divorced or things went wrong in their family. I even met one who was thrown out because his daughter died from a drug overdose – and he was the minister! He and his wife, already broken with grief, lost their income and their home, which came with the job. Please God, is this how we should show Your love to the world? Is this really what You died for, so that we could look down on others who are bloody and hurting and be critical of them? I often wonder why it is that we Christians throw the baby out with the bath water. We are surely the only army in the world who shoot our wounded. That is *not* our calling, but that has so often been my experience.

The result is often that the hurting person rejects the Church and therefore rejects God because of how they were treated. I meet people like that all the time. I even meet prison officers who say that the Church has hurt them in the past and they don't want to know God any more.

When I first became a Christian, I found the attitude of some people hard to deal with. Once, when I was speaking at a Christian event, I got threatened by someone wanting to kick my head in. This sometimes happened because of old enemies. On this occasion I told one of the Christian leaders and he said: 'It would be good for your humility, Brian.' Humility, I thought. You've got no idea how much I've been ground into the dust! You are completely clueless.

I knew that when I became a Christian, it was no more 'Mr Tough Guy'. God had to break me down and build me up again. However, he didn't make me into a puppet or a wind-up toy. I was still human, and it was hard to let go of some of who I was in the past. My T-shirt should have said, 'God's not finished with me yet'. I certainly beat myself up badly about my failings and I didn't need any one else's help to do that. But I got it anyway.

In the past I didn't care about anyone, but as a Christian, God made me very sensitive to other people. I found that silly things said to me would really hurt. For example, a rich guy I knew came to see us once and he gave me a five-pound note, telling me to make sure it went towards my family's needs and not on fags – at that time I still smoked. I can't begin to say how much that hurt. If someone has a need, I give in the name of the Lord and what they spend it on is down to them.

One of the things I've always had a problem with is my driving. I'd had years of tearing up the road at high speed as a Hell's Angel, but my love of speed didn't disappear overnight. I always wanted to be somewhere before I left. The journey meant little to me and it was getting there that mattered. When I was late or in a hurry, my foot would go down on the accelerator and my speed would go up.

It was good to know that I wasn't the only one who struggled with this. I remember going to a Christian conference once and at the end I came away racing to get home. My old car was clapped out, so I couldn't go too fast, but I was still breaking the speeding laws. And then suddenly some of these well-known Christian leaders zoomed by me in their posh cars at 90mph. That blew me away. It's not that I thought they were being hypocritical, just that they were being human.

Of course things like this would open me up to some very negative criticism from other Christians. In those early years I can recall someone saying to me: 'Brother, can I tell you something in love?' The slagging-off that followed was anything but love. I felt like saying to them: 'How do you think I felt when you hit me with that 'sledgehammer' and broke my heart? Where was the love in that, you total dipstick? Bog off!' No wonder that some of my guys from prison found it so hard to be a Christian on the out. It felt like there was always someone on our backs. Being a Christian isn't about having a go at each other. Who the heck would want to be in a family like that? God tells us to leave the judging to Him.

I do believe the truth has to be told. What I've found though is that rather than keeping people away from the Church, this sort of honesty has the opposite effect. People are so relieved that someone has opened up that area for discussion. Often if I've talked about this subject while preaching, there have been queues of people wanting to speak to me afterwards and tell me their painful story.

The reality is that the Church, with all its warts and blemishes, is filled with ordinary human beings who get it wrong, and at times they get it very badly wrong. But honesty and openness among Christian brothers and sisters is vital. It's not easy to be a Christian and we can be such hypocrites sometimes, acting like we're so nice and get it right all the time. If we are so busy acting, we are not a signpost to God, we are a lie. Just be honest about it! We want to be a light to those in darkness. This is what I want to be, but people sometimes look at me and say: 'He can't be a Christian if he's covered in tattoos, He's got that noisy trike, look at him, he's a nutter'. Yeah, too right I can be a nutter! I don't have the constraints of walking round in a suit, pretending to be something I'm not. God doesn't want anyone to pretend. I remember two Christian workers on the Isle of Dogs who deliberately dressed down when it wasn't normally their style, in order to 'relate' to people on the street. I mean, how insulting is that? It's like me painting myself black and going to talk to black guys in prison! We need to be real and be ourselves. I can be a nutter and still enjoy my life. It's about being transparent and honest and letting the light shine through me.

But being real can sometimes mean being hurt, misunderstood, blamed, rejected and isolated. However, even though other people and even members of the church may treat you like this, God never will. In fact one good thing I experienced during this dark and lonely period of my life was a deeper relationship and a new closeness with God.

Where I lived at the time, I had a fish pond with a seat by it where I sat for hours just crying. It was such a sad picture. But sitting there, staring into the water, feeling rejected and devastated, what I remember so vividly was the powerful presence of God as I struggled to come to terms with everything.

He said to me over and over: 'I'm with you, never will I leave you, never will I forsake you, Brian. You can swear, curse, get angry and I will still be here. No matter how deep your pain is, I will still be here. I will not walk away from you. I will never give up on you.'

I couldn't carry on with the ministry God had given me, so I pulled out of the prison work and did a number of normal jobs for a while until I got my head together. During that time I wrote a book which I called *The Life and Trials of Denby*. It was a fictitious historical prison story that was a total escape for me. It helped me through a tough time and pulled me away from the pain.

Eventually, I started to recover and told my trustee chairman that I wanted to get things going again. It was a bit tough at first because I was very fragile, but slowly I started to pull everything back together.

Because of what happened, it has taken me a long time to trust again. I was scarred and wary and certainly wasn't planning to meet anyone and remarry. However, there was someone who I had known for about eighteen years who was a respectable and 'boundaried' Christian lady. She helped me through some of that difficult period and we eventually fell in love and got married.

My wife is a psychotherapist, but she always had a heart to be a missionary. As a child she saw herself travelling around Africa on a bicycle, with a Bible under her arm and her hair in a bun. Then she meets an ex-Hell's Angel president and ends up in prison instead! But for fifteen years now she has been my soul mate, someone who I would trust with my life. We really do work as a team. She visits prisoners with me and at times when I preach she will play the hymns and do the Bible readings and prayers. It's a delight to have my wife by my side and whatever situation I walk into, she's right there with me.

We always share our day with each other and pray together

regularly. We invest a lot in our relationship and make sure that we spend at least one day a week together doing something as a couple – reading, fishing, going scuba diving, exploring the city and countryside. It gets better and better over the years. We have an honest relationship which is so important.

What I went through when my first marriage fell apart was horrendous. It cost me so very much, but I also learned so much through my pain. When God chose me, He knew that I was a fighter and no way was I going to give up on Him. Yet as a result of going through all that, I experienced a new closeness with God, ended up married to a fantastic woman and also gained another arrow in my quiver of arrows – something else that I could use to empathise with lads in prison and walk with them through their own suffering.

CHAPTER 12

At home and abroad

As a result of *Hell's Angel* going into different countries, I also started getting a lot of African prisoners writing to me. Their letters were so long, they were more like epistles! One of them who contacted me regularly was Jake. He was a lovely Christian guy and had been in a prison in Kabwe, Zambia, for a long time. One day, while reading one of his letters, I heard God's voice audibly over my left shoulder. 'Brian, I want you to go and see him.' I wanted to be obedient to God, so I told Christian friends that I needed to go to Zambia and they started donating money for the trip.

Then the horror stories started. So many people had a tale to tell about Zambia. Someone in my church told me that their son was held up by robbers with machine guns, who took everything and left him stood in the road in just his underpants. When I went for my jabs and told the doctor where I was going, he said, 'Oh no, my daughter went there,' and proceeded to tell me how terrible it had been. There were lots of encouragements like this!

I had no idea about what would happen when I got there or even who would be meeting me. I had written to the Prison Fellowship, who support prisoners and their families in this country and abroad, and was contacted by one of their team in Zambia. He was a former police officer who had done an armed robbery with machine guns, was sentenced and put on death row. He had later been released, I believe because of political activities by family and friends. In the end, when I arrived, I was met by this man from the Prison Fellowship who was related to the former Zambian ambassador.

It was quite a trek to the prison in Kabwe. The section where Jake was held was the maximum high security side, with high walls and guarded by officers with machine guns. Arriving at the gate, the guard looked at me and asked, 'What's your relationship with the prisoner?'

Blimey, I thought, they are not going to let me in. But he then looked down his list and said, 'Oh, you're a brother in Christ.'

I had worn white to reflect the African heat and keep me cool, and as I was escorted through the prison, I realised that all the prisoners were also dressed in white.

It was lovely to finally meet Jake and many of the other prisoners. The lads on death row, sentenced to execution, told me that every time they heard officers coming to their cell with their keys jangling, they had no idea whether they were about to be taken out and hanged. I preached in the chapel and twenty-seven of these men became Christians. I also had help from other Christian prisoners to distribute goods like clothing and books.

I visited some other prisons, for less serious offences. Some of these were only fenced in by barbed wire that prisoners could have easily stepped through, but they knew that if they tried, they would be immediately shot.

Travelling around the area, we passed a lot of copper mining and the huge Mukuyu Slave Tree, where slaves in the past had been bought and sold.

But there was another kind of trade that seemed to be thriving. Some of the hotels I stayed in were frequented by prostitutes trying to chat me up. I was appalled. 'On your bike! Go away! I'm a pastor,' I told them. Considering how I had felt about women, I wondered whether God was having a joke with me!

This trip was the only time I had taken my wedding ring off. I didn't want to show any jewellery because the risk of crime was everywhere and so many people had to be ready and armed. Visiting the British ambassador's house, with its high walls and twenty-four-hour guards, he showed me his collection of guns. He told me he would shoot on sight if someone tried to break in.

The trip lasted ten days altogether and God touched so many people. But what turned it sour was when I found out that the helper and host who escorted me was actually stealing from me. I had given him money for fuel on the way, and he was putting less fuel in and pocketing the rest. When he bought food for me, he always kept the change. I think he was also claiming money for the receipts from the Prison Fellowship, even though he hadn't paid for anything. I was so angry when I found this out. I grabbed hold of him, pinned him up against a wall and said, 'In my country, Christians do not do what you do. You do not steal from me!'

I made quite a few trips abroad like this because of the book, but back at home, the constant travelling meant that the ministry was starting to become a struggle. I had some of the best supporters you could possibly want as a full-time Christian worker and some have stayed with me for years. However, the cost of long journeys and hotels was becoming too much. It was exhausting at times. I had to realise that I wasn't Superman and couldn't do everything. It was time to start closing in on which prisons I would work in.

Up until the start of the new millennium, I had been visiting prisons for more than twenty years. But I had always attended as a visiting speaker and would be escorted through the prison to chapel and other places to speak to the lads. I had never been given my own keys to visit lads on the wings and in their cells. One day, when I was visiting Maidstone Prison in Kent, the chaplain, Rev Stephen Edwards, told me that he was going to be moving to the chaplaincy at Wandsworth, London's biggest prison. This was somewhere I had visited on rare occasions, over many years, but Stephen asked if I would be interested in doing some more work there and maybe being allocated keys. That's a joke, I thought. I knew the Bible said, 'All things are possible with God', but me, an ex-con with a record of violence, having prison keys? No chance!

But amazingly, Steve got me into Wandsworth on Sundays and I was cleared to have a full set of keys.

At first going back under the umbrella of the chaplaincy as a volunteer chaplain was tough. Not only was I used to working independently, but it brought back so many memories of when I was banged up there many years earlier. Looking out from what used to be the chapel window, I saw the old exercise yard marked out with concrete circles. It felt odd to remember walking around those circles as a prisoner. The visitors' section used to be the old Church of England chapel where I have preached a number of times since. I walked into the laundry room and it hit me like a hammer when I suddenly remembered working there. Memories flooded back of fights that had happened in that room, which was now the domain of the VPU (Vulnerable Prisons' Unit) prisoners, the sex offenders who would be attacked if they were on the main wing. I chatted to the prisoners in that section and told them that I remembered working there. By the looks on their faces, I could see they thought I was a sex case. I had to explain quickly that things had changed since then.

But I realised just how much I was wrapped up in a miracle, that God had brought me to this place. I'd done bird here and suddenly here I am walking around unescorted and unlocking doors. I remember one day we had the 'burglars' in – security staff who wanted to spin the chapel – and they were asking me to unlock doors to cupboards that they didn't have the keys for;

me, an ex-con, unlocking doors for security! Wow, I thought. This is really good.

Most of my work involved seeing new prisoners in reception, talking to lads who were suicidal or responding to those who had asked to see a chaplain. However, what made this work difficult was that a little while after joining the team, security came back with their check on me and suddenly I lost my cell key. This was probably the most important of all the keys, because without it I wasn't able to freely go into cells and talk to men face-to-face. It seemed that despite their desires to see prisoners rehabilitated, those in the prison system were putting barriers in the way of the ones who were trying to help

This decision meant extra work for the officers who had to unlock each cell door for me, bang the bolt to spring the lock so that I couldn't be taken hostage and leave me to speak in private. When I had finished, they had to come back and lock the prisoner up again. I still felt that I sometimes had to prove myself to the staff, being an ex-con. There were a few that were helpful but sometimes, as soon as I came onto the wing, some staff would disappear and I was on my own, with no one to help. This meant that if I wanted to speak to a prisoner, I was forced to talk to him through the cell doors. This was hard work because of the noise on the wings and we couldn't really hear each other.

It was extremely frustrating and after some months it really started to get to me. I wondered if I should give up for a while and wait for full clearance. I decided to appeal to the number one governor heading up the prison and attended an interview with him, accompanied by Steve, the chaplain. I took all the newspaper and magazine articles, positive comments and reviews that had been written about me to demonstrate to him the genuine change in my life and my desire to help prisoners. I presented myself well, but not well enough. There was no moving the governor because my crimes had been so bad. My last sentence on paper had been twelve years. He also queried why the chaplain was accompanying me because he didn't think I needed his help.

The governor asked me to leave my request for keys with him and he would see how things went. But nothing happened. Steve was always in my corner and had a word with one of the other governors in security he knew – there were five altogether in Wandsworth. The result was that eight months later I was given a full set of keys and finally felt like a fully-launched member of the chaplaincy team! Since then, I have also been cleared to have keys for High Down and Coldingley prisons, although in Coldingley I don't need a cell key for the work that I do.

I am not a natural team man, much more of a loner, preferring to work by myself. But in the years that I have been going into Wandsworth, I have tried my best to work with the rest of the staff. The guys I used to call 'screws' I now respect as professional officers and call them 'sir' or 'ma'am', with no problem at all. Most of the officers call me Brian. The work is tough, but I love it.

Working with reception prisoners is often a challenge because you never know what sort of state they will be in or how they are going to react to the shock of prison. In truth I don't believe today's prisons are hard places: many prisoners have their own television and Game Boys, there are usually only two to a cell instead of three, they have more rights and have to be treated with more respect now – otherwise the prisoner can take prisons to court for the failure of such rights. In my day you couldn't even be seen speaking to a prison officer because you would be accused of 'grassing' and get a kicking from other prisoners.

However, new prisoners are often in a painful and difficult place during these early days. Sometimes they would still be drunk, out of their heads on drugs, very angry at being given a long sentence or have mental health issues. Their crimes may have been widely publicised, they could be dealing with friends and family turning against them or losing their jobs and homes.

I talk to them, find out what their needs are and mention any concerns to staff if I feel they are a possible danger to themselves or others. I feel it is my place to warn them. I remember alerting staff to one new prisoner that I felt could be a danger to them. An hour or so later I was working down the block, checking on the lads there when a prisoner was brought in, bent over and held by officers. 'You were right, Brian,' the officers said. It was the guy I had warned them about. He had just attacked someone.

Every day I hear stories of men who have been through much the same as I did in my childhood years and have now given up on themselves. Once I was speaking to a number of reception prisoners when a young black lad approached me. He looked so down, almost in tears. He told me that he had worked in television, made some big mistakes and couldn't believe that God would forgive him.

'Let's ask Him,' I said. I placed my hands on him and prayed for him, then told him to pray out loud, just so that I knew when he had finished. There were a number of prisoners watching and checking us out. When he finished praying, his face lit up. It was as though I saw the glory of God in him. What had happened to that tearful, broken man of a few minutes ago? He'd recognised his need for God, reached out and then – wham! – the Holy Spirit does His thing.

I always like to check out how genuine these men are, although in the end only God knows where they are at. But I have seen and experienced too many who have claimed to be Christians and yet end up back in prison. I never believe in making it easy for them, because in my experience it is not easy to live a Christian life. I often pray for them in front of their friends and if they are afraid of that, then I know that they will struggle as a Christian in prison as well as on the out.

Once when I was talking and praying with a prisoner on a wing, another came up interrupting me and asked, 'Can you help me? I want to be a Christian.'

'Yeah, sure you do,' I said, grinning at him. I thought that if he walked away from me now, he wasn't as keen or genuine about knowing God as he claimed. So I ignored him and carried on talking to the first prisoner while watching this other guy out of the corner of my eye. He didn't know what to make of my response, but he waited for me.

When I had finished with the first prisoner, I turned to him and said, 'Tell me about it.' He explained that his parents were missionaries abroad and how ashamed he was of being in prison. I could feel his hurt and shame and so together we prayed for forgiveness and for Jesus to come into his life.

Sometimes I am able to keep in touch with guys once they are released. One of them, Lennox, was a cleaner on C wing and I think he was a Christian when I first met him. He was a special guy and together we tried to look after the lads on the wing. He was able to tell me about some guys who were searching for meaning in their lives and others who were feeling a bit fragile. On release, he moved to the East End of London, married a lovely Christian girl, Bali, and they started a ministry working with local gangs. Lennox is a big black lad with designs cut into his very short hair and really relates to the kids on the streets. He and his wife often take groups of these young people into prison to show the reality of where a life of crime, drugs and violence can lead to.

Another guy I met after he was released from prison was Brian, who used to live down in Devizes. He reminded me of my own past life. He had been involved in gang fights and had his head done in with drugs. He is now married with two children and for a while ran a Christian drug rehabilitation centre. He was able to make a lot of positive changes in the unit and be firm with the men, setting good boundaries. Eventually, he left and trained as a mental health nurse.

There are a lot of guys I work with who will be locked up for many years, especially those in for murder. This does mean though that I am able to offer individual counselling to them over a longer period. This is often the case in High Down prison. I spent about three years working there with one man who was in for murder. He really felt that he had screwed up his life, but he was totally cut off from his feelings when I first met him. Every time I talked about God, he would look uncomfortable and change the subject. It reminded me of what I used to be like, not letting people close to me. I encouraged him over the years to try and express how he felt.

As he was getting close to his case review, he asked if I would go with him. I knew that I wouldn't get a chance to speak on his behalf, but I decided to write a letter to the judge in support of him. When we went up for the review, supported by myself and one of his long-term Christian friends, I was amazed as I listened to him talk. He was honest with the judge about how he was feeling, which I knew was very hard for him. He was sent off to a Category D prison, for less serious offences, to prepare him for his release, which was a great move for him. I know that on the out he continued to have the support of Christian friends.

In all my years of prison work, I have found that many murderers can be really nice guys. Usually, like me, their lives have been so screwed up, so full of pain and frustration, that it had to come out somewhere, somehow. They then end up in even worse pain living with the guilt and remorse that they have taken someone's life, and find themselves serving a life sentence.

One of these guys who I worked with was a lovely lad called Tony. He had killed his two close friends and I worked with him every week over a long period. He became a Christian, but what hit me hard was that I would be dead before Tony is due to be released as his sentence carries such a long tariff.

It's hard for guys facing a long sentence like this, but at least I know that God will be with them through it. I remember a couple of lads on remand who I met in Wandsworth in 2009. I had just gone onto A wing to see a prisoner who I found out was a pastor. There are all sorts of people in prison: counsellors, magistrates, vicars, police. I'm not really interested in their past work or what their crime is, because I know whatever it is, God can deal with it.

I wasn't really sure what he wanted, but we flipped through the Bible and talked about how God blesses us. In the country he had come from, pastors are very prestigious and I think he had been given a hard time because of his crime. He just needed a blessing from the Bible on that day.

As I came out of his cell, I locked his door and turned around to be confronted by two 'rottweilers', Roger and Lenny. I'm six feet tall and weigh about nineteen stone, and these guys were bigger in every sense. They were brothers who shared a cell.

'Brian, can we talk to you? Can you come over to our cell?' I went with them and they showed me a copy of the Trust leaflet that tells my story and how God has changed my life.

'Look, we were out on the exercise yard and saw this on the ground,' they said. 'That's what we want. We want to be Christians.'

I thought at first that maybe they were having a laugh, but they were too big to laugh at! They told me that they were gypsies who had been involved in bare knuckle fighting. As I listened to them, I could see that they were very serious. God really takes me by surprise at times! So in cell 3.16 on A wing, both men prayed that God would come into their lives, forgive them and help them to be the men that he wanted them to be.

Over the next few weeks and months I watched these men and tried to get to see them when I could. It wasn't too hard to track them down because they both worked on their wing. Roger and Lenny quickly became known by the staff as straight and reliable men. They didn't get involved in anything they shouldn't and their witness of changed behaviour spoke for them.

After a very long time of being on remand, they told me that there was no way that as Christians they could lie in court. They were going to put their hands up and tell the truth to the judge. They were found guilty and sentenced. I had thought that they both would get about eight years, but in fact one got thirteen and the other fourteen years. I felt so devastated for them and didn't really know what to say. As soon as I was able, I went round to see them. They were very quiet. It had hit them hard, but their faith has carried them through it. Just because someone becomes a Christian in prison, it doesn't mean that they will be let off from what they have done, because we all have to face the consequences of our actions. But I do know that they will have spiritual help throughout their sentence.

Both of these guys are now in Parkhurst Prison on the Isle of Wight and still walking with the Lord. They continue to have an excellent reputation with staff because of their faith. I feel very proud of them.

Working with men classed as dangerous doesn't worry me. This isn't me being arrogant, as some people have said, but I always feel that God is very close to me whatever the situation I find myself in, and because of that I know His peace. It's very important for someone in my position to have good prayer support and I am blessed with a great church and a committed circle of supporters, who have seen their prayers answered over and over again. I have only been attacked twice in the thirty-two years of working in prisons, but I still need to be careful and have an awareness of what is happening around me. I have done some martial arts training, but I have no need to get into fights.

For years, there's been a special communication between me and God in prisons, so much so that I know almost instantly which guys God is going to work on. I can look at them and think: you're marked and you're marked. I go back later and pray with them and see each one become a Christian.

Sometimes officers warn me to keep away from certain prisoners who are violent, but I know if God wants me to see them He will protect me. In fact, God often seems to pick the toughest guys for me to work with, who are usually the ones who need the most help. But I just look at these men and think that the guy I'm working for is bigger than the one you're working for! What do I have to fear?

CHAPTER 13

Delight and devastation

One day when I went to see a new prisoner in A Wing in Wandsworth, I was surprised to see five prison officers standing on his landing. I informed them, as I always do, that I was working there and told them who I had come to see.

'Have you got a cell key?' I was asked. I told them I had.

'Well, be careful of him. I would leave him if I were you,' they warned. 'He has already threatened to throw a number of staff over the top.' This sounded like a charming guy!

'But I have to see him – he's a reception prisoner,' I explained.

One of the group, a small-built lady officer, said that she would go with me. I smiled at that. None of the other, bigger officers had offered. I didn't feel afraid, so told her I would be OK on my own. I peeped in his door as we always have to, checking on potential suicides or respecting toilet privacy. He was sitting down calm and close to the door, writing something. Opening the door I said, 'Chaplain.' He looked at me amazed and grabbed a letter from the top bunk.

'Look, I was just going to write to ask to see you,' he said.

'So before you asked, God has answered,' I said. He looked at me and started to cry. Mark was a tough-looking guy who had been round the block a few times. He told me that he had been slung out of Australia where his dad, a real tough guy, was a diamond miner. Mark had previously had a good education, but was now hooked on class A drugs and his life was in a mess. As is often the way, when Mark had gone to court he had taken loads of drugs beforehand, so when he came to prison he was out of his head and very violent.

He had come to the end of his tether and knew he needed help. There was only one place for him to go now, I thought. He needed God. I challenged him with the gospel, telling him about Jesus and about my own life. Crying, he asked for God's forgiveness and asked Him to come into his life and help him to be the man that He wanted him to be.

Leaving the cell and going back past the staff who had warned me of him, I grinned at them and said nothing. I so wanted to tell them what had happened, but if this was for real they would see the difference in him for themselves.

I kept an eye on Mark, as I do with all new Christians in prison. I was due to take a service in the chapel soon and an idea started bubbling around in my brain. What if Mark was willing to stand with me and give his testimony? I asked Steve, the chaplain, for permission and he agreed, but he was a bit concerned about what might happen, which is understandable. It's not normally a good idea to pick a prisoner out and make him the focus of attention among the rest of the prisoners.

On that morning, I invited Mark to come to the front and tell us about what was going on in his life. Mark started speaking to the men in a very low tone, telling them what he used to be like and how different he was as a Christian.

'Speak up, speak up,' someone shouted. I watched Mark. He just continued telling the guys quietly about his new-found faith. I smiled, remembering him telling me that he had studied psychology. He had thought about it and perhaps the only way for the guys to hear him was by being very quiet. It worked – you could have heard a pin drop! When he finished the guys stood up and clapped him. It was wonderful!

I told the chaplain, Steve, what had happened with Mark and he was thrilled. I have had a lot of good support from chaplains over the years, but there are some in chaplaincy teams who don't seem to give a positive response to guys becoming Christians. It's between them and God, though. For me, I find it a real joy to be part of what God is doing in prisons. This is the God who created the world and said, 'Let there be light' and here He is using me to help change lives. It's amazing!

One of the places I have always loved doing chaplains' duties is down the block. The CSU (Care and Segregation Unit), also known as the 'seg', is where the dangerous and more violent or seriously disturbed prisoners are taken. The unit in Wandsworth holds around fourteen prisoners and they are watched carefully and assessed, often to be shipped out to a more secure prison. When I was banged up, this was a place of fear where there were rumours of beatings and mistreatment. Nowadays it's different, with plenty of CCTV around, making sure that if anyone – prisoners or staff – claimed to be beaten up or attacked, the truth would show on camera.

I have to be very careful to work with the staff because of the nature of the men. Once I've signed my time in and made a list of prisoners, I get updates from the staff about the guys there before I go round and talk to them, as you never know what sort of response you will get. At times some prisoners would be in such a bad place that it would not be appropriate for me to go in. Some are on a three-man or maybe even a five-man unlock (the number of officers needed to deal with a prisoner at any one time) because of their unpredictable and dangerous behaviour. Even if I felt it was appropriate to talk to these guys, it would mean that the staff would have to put on their riot gear before I even opened the cell door.

Other times you can open a door and get faeces thrown at you when prisoners are on a 'dirty protest'. This is when they smear themselves, the walls and floors with their own excrement, making them untouchable.

Steve, who showed me the ropes, always told me to take as much time as I needed when working here, because these are the guys who are usually in the greatest need of help. I have often walked around the exercise yard with a prisoner down the seg, which always amazes them that I am willing to do so.

I have to say that this is an area in the prison where the staff really shine through. It's a tough job, and can be a very negative one for them. It is a place where I have always felt supported by officers and often I am impressed by the care and support they show to the prisoners.

Part of our work is to see men who are placed on an ACCT (Assessment, Care in Custody and Teamwork), who have threatened to self-harm or to kill themselves. They often cannot cope with their situation or what they have done, and feel that they need the help and attention that being on a self-harm watch brings them. I remember going to see one such guy. He told me he was determined to kill himself because he couldn't take any more. We talked for a long time and when I said goodbye and walked out of the door, he said, 'Brian, can you put me down for chapel on Sunday?' I nearly burst out laughing. This was a guy who was going to kill himself as soon as I shut his door!

Another time I went to see a prisoner who had requested to see a chaplain. As I talked to him, I noticed that his cell mate was crying. He had a piece of paper in his hand.

'Are you all right?' I asked in concern.

He showed me his bit of paper. It was a letter to his mum saying that he was going to kill himself. I believed that this lad was very serious. I tried talking to him, but I wasn't getting through.

'OK, I need to take you down to see the senior officer,' I told him. There was no way I was going to walk away from him. I generally get on well with staff, but this SO – a big guy covered in tattoos – was someone I didn't know too well. He looked well hard and not the sort to mess with. I explained what was going on and showed him the letter. While I was with him, the SO phoned through to the governor, who asked him if he thought it was serious. 'The chaplain thinks so, sir,' he said. I knew I could leave it with this good man, and the governor was on the way to sort it out. God calls and equips us, but He often uses different methods to help those we work with.

All of us are affected when prisoners try to kill themselves and we have seen it all too often. I remember hearing a female prison officer scream one day near to my office. I rushed out and saw staff running towards a cell where there was a disturbance going on. I thought that some guy had attacked her and I felt the urge to hit out at this prisoner as he was escorted past me. This is not a normal reaction from me now, but that's how affected I was by it, even though I knew I'd be thrown out of the prison if I did.

Then I saw the doctor come flying along the landing and understood what had happened. A prisoner had tried to hang himself. The medical staff worked on him for a long time. It was a close call, but they saved his life.

Sadly, we are not able to save them all. Some of them were just too determined to die, unable to cope with the pain of their past and things they had done wrong. One of these was James, someone we got to know well in Winchester. James was a well-known prisoner who had hit the national press headlines for killing his gay lover. Over about fourteen months, through letters and face-to-face meetings, he told me his story. He shared the pain of his home life. His drunken father would come home, spitting smoky and boozy breath as he shouted into his face. As well as dealing with the brutality of his dad, his older brother always blamed James for anything that went wrong.

His lover had walked away from him and it had broken him,

resulting in the murder. James was a very special person and a very sensitive man who was well liked by his fellow prisoners and staff. But he was also eaten up with his guilt and grief. The pain of his rejection and abuse had led him to his own destruction.

One Wednesday evening, we were getting ready to go down to Winchester when we had a phone call from the chaplain. He told me that James had killed himself. Everyone in the prison was devastated. He still wanted us to come down, but asked if we could help with a service of remembrance for James.

That evening in the chapel we thanked God for the real man we had known, a gentle and passive man who had finally been pushed too far. It was as if the whole of his pain burst out of him and he found himself in custody, having to face up to something which was destroying him.

Ben was another special lad who couldn't take any more and wanted to die. He was in the hospital wing in Wandsworth, refusing to eat and slowly starving himself to death. I visited him regularly and he would show me cards from his family. I sat on his bed hour after hour talking about how much his family loved him and the pain it would cause them if he died. I told him about the suicides I had known, the effect on staff and prisoners, the flowers at the gates outside left by devastated family and friends. I did everything I could to bring him to the place where he could begin to care about himself and his family.

This was during the summer and we had a brief holiday down in the West Country. When I came back to work that Monday I was feeling refreshed, recharged and ready for anything. I went straight over to the healthcare block to check on Ben. His bed was empty. I asked a nurse where he was and she told me that I needed to report to the office. There I found out that Ben had died a few days earlier. I was devastated. This poor kid with so many hang-ups, so many problems going round in his head, had copped out, perhaps with little thought for his family who loved him so much. He'd had enough. I just wish he could have experienced having God in his life, known healing from the hurts and found out what it was like to be truly loved. He missed out on so much.

Perhaps these men didn't know God, but sometimes even Christians can make terrible mistakes and get to the point where they can't take any more. One ex-prisoner and a man I had a great relationship with was Bob. I don't know how he came to faith, but Bob came out of prison as a Christian. We became good friends, we were brothers in Christ and I certainly had a lot of empathy for him.

Bob got involved with his local church doing voluntary work, and they took him under their wing and encouraged him in his faith and direction. I was surprised to hear that Bob wanted to be an ordained Anglican minister, which is a hard job to do, but he got through his studies and his ordination, moved to a church in the south of England, married and had a family. He arranged for me to speak at a meeting in his area and we also met with an ex-con who I knew from the local prison. Bob was doing his best to serve God.

However, some months later I heard that Bob had suffered a mental breakdown and was in a Christian retreat trying to get his head back into a better place. A year later I learnt that he had taken his own life by hanging himself.

I have no doubt that Bob was a changed man and one who wanted to serve God. But I understand that he did something that he was deeply ashamed of and couldn't live with the guilt and pain. To be honest, I felt so angry with Bob and wanted to smack him if I could, yet that wasn't what he had needed. It was love and support, not judgment. I have to say too that I was amazed at how some Christians talked to me about Bob after his death, as if he had failed in some way. They seemed to be lacking love or empathy for him.

A year after Bob had killed himself, it was coming up to Christmas and I was doing my rounds down the seg. I peeped through the spy hole in one cell door and saw a young prisoner hanging. Sounding the alarm, the staff came running and quickly cut him down. I looked at the prisoner's name. It was exactly the same surname as my mate Bob's. What's going on, God? I thought. I don't need this. The memories of Bob and his sad ending came flooding back. So often it has been my past pain, failures and hurts that God has used when I am working with broken people. It's as if none of what we go through, no matter how painful, is wasted.

But on this occasion, it didn't end in tragedy. Several weeks later I was with my wife in the prison. I always get shocked looks from the lads when I say, 'Well, I did promise her a day out!' We chatted to various guys and went to healthcare to visit the prisoner who I had found hanging. He was sitting on a bench in the exercise yard and we could still see the blue-black bruising around his throat from the rope. We tried to offer words of comfort and support, but he was out of it on medication and had no idea who we were or what day of the week it was.

Even now, many years after some of these tragic events have taken place, it still hurts and I ask myself if there was something – anything – that I could have done or said that would have helped these guys. I'm sure I did my best at the time, but why on earth didn't they open up, talk to me about their pain and let me help them? Sadly for some, the pain is so unbearable that it seems death is the only way out. For them and for us, their suicide is the ultimate rejection of any help.

One thing all this has taught me, though – which hit me after my friend Mark Birchall died of cancer – was how important it is to say things to people's faces while I still have the chance, even if it embarrasses them. I tell my wife every day how much

I love her – even when I'm preaching! Tim Bryan, the number-one chaplain at Wandsworth, said to me recently, 'Cor I'm going to miss your ugly face when you retire!' I responded by telling him what a lovely man he was and that I have the utmost respect for him. I think it's important to tell people how valuable they are while you still can. Who knows what tomorrow may bring?

In all the years I've worked in prisons, God has not only used me to reach prisoners, but also to bring others into the work. In fact, Tim, a retired senior police officer and one of my former trustees, joined the chaplaincy team after coming with me on a prison visit.

'So, what is it you actually do in prison?' he asked me one day.

'Well, I work with reception prisoners,' I said.

'What's reception?'

'It's where new prisoners come in. I also go down the block ...'

'What's the block?'

Well it's ... oh blimey, why don't you come in with me and see?'

So he did. He thought I drove quite fast, though! He was a 'fly on the wall' for the day, observing everything. One guy we saw in his cell offered us coffee. We tried to protest because we didn't want to take his supplies, but he insisted. I was able to lead him to the Lord that day with Tim, not knowing that this prisoner was a Muslim.

Later, in the office, we met the chaplain, Gordon, who said to Tim that he had a new vacancy for a resettlement chaplain. Would he be interested?

Driving home, Tim was reading the job description and suddenly shouted: 'Yes, this is for me!' He got the job and got on really well with everyone. Later, when the job for the number-one chaplain came up, he applied and got that too, even though there's no way that someone with his lack of experience in the prison system would normally get a job like this. He is a great chaplain and encourager to the men.

Someone else who is now involved in prison work, who was also one of my trustees, is Chris Moore. He is now the chief executive of the Clink Charity, which operates The Clink restaurant in High Down, run by prisoners for the general public. They are trained in catering and promised a job on the out. It's been on TV and in the newspapers, and is so successful they're rolling it out to other prisons. Chris recently wrote to me: 'It was through you that I became interested in prisons and it was my heart operation that made me rethink my career and what life is all about.'

So God uses me in amazing ways and I do feel a bit embarrassed talking like this, because it sounds like I'm boasting. But I don't have much to boast about. It's only God that keeps me from being what I used to be and what I could so easily become again.

CHAPTER 14

The monster contained

A few years ago I was speaking in a midweek church meeting about how God was changing prisoners' lives, when an elderly man jumped up, virtually foaming at the mouth.

'Can I say something?' he said.

'Yes, of course,' I told him, thinking that this could be interesting!

'I'm shocked,' he said angrily. 'I'm shocked that you can say that those sorts of people can know God. How can people like that be saved?'

I didn't say much at the time, but I could so easily have! I was tempted to say, 'Well, isn't it nice to be so wrong? Jesus was a prisoner who was beaten up and put on trial. What about Judas who grassed Him up and Peter who cut off someone's ear and denied knowing Him? And I'm an ex-con. Are you shocked that I could be saved? I've done more in my years as a Christian for God than you would ever know!'

But it wasn't worth humiliating him in order to correct him. He wasn't very spiritually bright, but he was being honest about where he was coming from, which was a very ignorant place. Someone else could put him right another day.

In some ways I can understand how he feels. I don't tend to judge prisoners for what they have done; it's not my place to do so. But there have been times when I've worked with someone or led him to the Lord, gone home, looked him up on the internet and found out about the horrific crimes he's committed. It's painful reading. I often say to God: 'How can You save someone so awful and evil?' But then I see myself as I once was – a sick and evil animal. I hurt and injured so many people. I attacked without provocation, chain-whipping some, smashing into the faces of others with a helmet, slashing rivals with knives and other vicious weapons and nearly murdering two lads by stabbing them in the guts. I once blinded someone with a broken beer bottle who was already lying injured on the road. He had come to the pub looking for a fight and I had knocked him to the ground, jumped up in the air, landed on his face and ground broken glass into his eyes. Another time a man followed me around at work doing a time and motion study that I didn't know about, so I cornered him, grabbed him by the hair and stabbed him in the throat.

When I think about God loving me, it moves me to tears because I'm such a horrible person really. If anyone stands up at my funeral and says that I was a good man and a lovely guy, I've told my wife to hit them! I'm not a good man. I'm a bad man that God uses. I want to be known as a man of God who tried to do the best he could. But I don't do things to impress people. I don't visit prisoners so that people will think I'm a good guy; that would make me vomit! I'd rather be dead than be what people want me to be.

Even though it devastates me to think about what I have done in the past, I know God uses it all to reach guys in prison. Before I knew God I was totally cut off from emotion, but when I became a Christian, suddenly my emotions were thrown wide open and when I talk to guys, I can feel their pain with them. God uses my feelings and emotions to relate to people. But He also uses the things that I've done. For example in Wandsworth I was talking to a prisoner who was in a really bad place mentally. I was talking about God being the answer and he said, 'God can't possibly forgive me for what I've done.'

I started telling him about some of the awful things in my past, including stabbing an innocent man in the throat. This lad looked at me, gobsmacked and said: 'I'm in here for killing someone. I cut his throat.' I didn't know anything about this at the time. He was able to relate to me and I could communicate with him.

It comes at a cost. Not many people truly understand that. There have been so many who have been desperate to hear my testimony and some, mainly women, would say to me: 'Oh I wish I had a testimony like yours – it's so wonderful!' And I would think to myself, 'You're in cuckoo land, girl!' They just didn't understand where I was coming from. Did they have any idea how painful it was to have my dad walk away, my family reject me and my mum abuse and hate me? Did they understand the total confusion of my life? Did they know how miserable and damaged I was and about the uncontrollable anger that nearly destroyed me? Don't water it down, speak the truth. Why on earth would they want my testimony?

And sometimes when I gave a talk about my past, someone would ask a crazy question like: 'So, do you miss your days as a Hell's Angel then?' What? Are you having a laugh? Every day was one of explosive anger, violence, misery, drugs, crime and loneliness. How could I possibly miss that? Haven't you heard anything I've been saying?

I get upset when I hear some testimonies from new Christians, though. I heard one on Premier Christian Radio a while ago and the guy was glorifying his past life and saying: 'I used to be ever so rich. I had five or six cars, I had loads of women. And then I became a Christian.'

What? Is that it? Well, sounds like you're a bit of a mug, mate. Why did you give up all that? He didn't explain just how wonderful it is to be a Christian, how amazing it is to know you're forgiven. Why would people not want to shout about that? Every day I experience God's love and forgiveness and the excitement of life with Him. So my walk with God is far from boring; it's always new and challenging. In fact I feel sorry for other people who don't have God in their life.

Yet I am also very aware that it's only His power keeping me from going back to what I used to be. I can lose my temper in an instant and it's from one to ten immediately, as many people are aware.

I recently asked for some advice on eating healthily from a dietician to try and keep my weight down. She tried to tell me what food I couldn't eat and I started getting angry. At one time I barely had enough to eat.

'Don't you tell me what I can and can't eat,' I told her.

'Oh, you're *that* Brian Greenaway are you?'

But it's more than just losing my temper. Inside, that very dysfunctional part of me hasn't gone. It's still there, in my nature. If I'm pushed I want to attack and there's a massive destruction button in me. I know how the monster grows and comes out because I've experienced it. I know what the agony of rejection and abuse can do to people. Many would say that they don't know how a guy can tear through a town shooting everyone, as we sometimes see in the media. Well I know, because I have felt that intense pain and anger. It has to come out somehow. I see guys in prison regularly who self-harm and they are suffering so much that they rip their arms to bits. They are trying to say to the world: 'Look! This is how much it hurts!'

The monster in me is really powerful and there have been many situations when I felt that I could have easily killed people. I wanted to, but they didn't die and it's only by God's grace and mercy. I've seen lads in prison for murder who have been in fights like me, who sometimes were nowhere near as bad as me. They are locked up for life. That should have been me so many times over. But if that had happened, I couldn't have gone into the prison work God planned for me. He was in control of it all, even before I knew Him.

Now God is the one who is in control and He does not let me get into situations that I would have previously fired up in and caused destruction, even right back in the early days when I wanted to kill a screw over a budgie! The monster inside is well subdued. If God ever took that lid off, my life would be over. I would end up dead or in prison for a long time. Please God, contain me. Don't ever let this happen! I do believe that God is always watching over me and protecting me. But it's more than that. He's protecting me from myself.

I continue to do my best and be available to God to use me in the way that He wants. It's hard to be a real Christian, especially when stuff starts hitting you in the face and really hurts. What do you do? Do you smash someone in the mouth, crack up or brush yourself down and get on with it?

I'm well aware of my weaknesses. I was at a tent crusade many years ago and a guy laid hands on me and said what he believed God was saying: 'You will be a Peter for me.' That's really nice of him, I thought. Peter was a disciple of Jesus and I'm going to be like him!

Then I went home and read more about Peter. I found out he was a bit of a yo-yo – up one minute and down the next. Yep, that's me! I could relate because I have suffered from depression for many years and nothing takes away the awfulness of that. I have other health problems like tinnitus and gout. But I still want to be in the place that God wants me to be in and every day I say to Him: 'Here I am, Lord, available for You.'

Any suffering is nothing compared to what God did for us. I was recently helping a friend in the garden. There we were, these two old men throwing sand and cement into a mixer when we really don't have the energy for such physical work anymore. My friend suffers from back problems and he was in great pain doing the work. But he suddenly said: 'God, You sent Your son to die for us. Why should I have it easy?' He's right. Despite my problems, nothing compares to what Jesus went through.

Jesus didn't die on a cross only for the good people. He died for the unlovely people, like me. Nobody should think they are too good for that or better than the guys in prison. So often Christians say: 'There but by the grace of God go I.' I often wonder if they really understand what they are saying. I know I do. I'm living proof of that.

And yet, despite all the proof, there are still those who refuse to believe the truth of what really happened to me.

CHAPTER 15

Fact or Fiction?

I stood there in shock, looking at the young girl who had just spoken to me. I couldn't believe what I was hearing.

'Your book isn't true. My auntie said so.'

I was visiting my former school, Petersfield Secondary Modern (now the Petersfield School). I had been invited by a Christian teacher to speak to a number of classes throughout the day. I guess that he had heard about me or read my book and thought that being a former pupil, maybe telling my story would be a good Christian challenge to his classes.

I had spent the day telling and re-telling my story, which I was prepared to do, but always hated doing. Every time I talk about my past, all the painful memories and emotions come flooding back and it hurts all over again. Opening up old wounds drains me of energy, but I believe God has allowed this so that I can have real empathy with guys in prison.

At the end of the school day, most of the kids rushed off, leaving me with the teacher and one of the pupils. As we walked out of the Portakabin classroom, the teacher told me with an odd grin that this girl had a question to ask me.

In truth I was expecting something thoughtful or even spiritual. But when she told me what her auntie had apparently said, I was stunned. My jaw must have hit the ground. The shock wasn't from the statement, it was because I had known her auntie as a kid and heard that she had died years ago. I later wondered if I had got her and her sister mixed up.

I didn't respond at the time, but because of my reaction, it must have looked as if I'd been caught out. But I'd told my story a number of times already throughout the day and not been questioned. If anyone was challenging the truth of what I was saying, they could have brought it up at any point in the day.

I went home fuming. What did her aunt know, or come to that, what did anyone know about what went on in our home when we were children? I was being called a liar by a school kid and supporting her in this was this so-called Christian teacher! Where was he coming from? Why should I put myself through the pain of bringing up my past just to be criticised, misunderstood and accused of lying by thoughtless people with no understanding?

I suspected at the time that he believed I was exaggerating my testimony to glorify the good old days. But that was the complete opposite of where I was coming from. Some of the things I did were so awful that I would try and say them less graphically, because it's not nice to hear.

Yet again I had the same feeling of not being listened to and not being believed. It reminded me of the attitude shown by the uneducated, moronic people I had grown up with in my home village, putting me down and accusing me of lies. If I was lying, how hard is it to look through records and newspaper cuttings of my crimes against society? And there have been a lot of them! The truth was there for those who wanted to find it.

Perhaps one of the ways I deal with my anger is to talk it out and write it out, as you can see by reading this. But there were times when I wondered if I had exaggerated my childhood in my memory. Was it really as bad as I thought? Was the hill I struggled up with half a hundredweight of coal as an eight-year-old really as steep as I'd imagined?

To find out the truth, and also to show my wife where I grew up, we revisited Steep, my childhood home. And yes, the hill I struggled up was as bad as I had thought back then.

I also went back to the place where the blacksmith used to work, where I spent time as a child. It's a cycle shop now. We visited the site of the old farm where me and my sisters, feeling very hungry, were given bread and dripping by the farmer's wife and we spotted my auntie in the street where I grew up, looking out of the window at us. She's a white-haired old lady now who seems to live on her own.

I still had so many unanswered questions in my head about my childhood, particularly about my dad and why he left. One day I received a phone call from the publishers of my first book to say that a woman called Greenaway had been trying to get in touch. They gave me her phone number and left it up to me to contact her.

I decided to phone and see what it was all about. She told me her name and that we shared the same dad. He had recently died and up until then she had known nothing about me or my sisters or that he'd ever been married before. Sounds like the usual Greenaway game!

We eventually met up with her and her husband and had lunch together. She told me about her brother dying a few years ago and that her dad was a well-respected man in the community. So much so that at his funeral, all the local people came out of their houses and shops to pay their respects as the funeral procession went by. I had to bite my tongue. This was not the dad that I had grown up not knowing. If he was such a good guy, how come his oldest – and now only – surviving son wasn't at his funeral? And how come his children never knew that he had been married before?

My half-sister went on to tell me that her dad had said to the family that he had been working hard so he could send money to us. But working out the dates, the time he said he was supposed to be sending money was when we were all adults and had left home. He rarely, if ever, sent money for us as children. I know it's going to shock her to read what's in this book about him, but I can't lie to her about it. I can only be honest about his neglect and behaviour towards us and how it was for me.

At one time I had plotted to kill my dad, because I believed he needed to know fatally how much he had damaged me. But when I became a Christian, there wasn't the need for revenge any more; there was no need to tell him how angry I was. It still would have been lovely to sit in a room with him and talk to him man to man about what happened and to finally have some understanding and answers to questions I have had since childhood. I know that they will never be answered now, but my life has moved on.

My strong feelings about honesty have also meant that I have no relationship with my mother. I have forgiven her for the way she treated me and my sisters, but I still feel very angry that she discounts everything that happened and refused to believe one of my sisters when she told her about the abuse that had occurred. For years I didn't want anything to do with her because I didn't believe that I could have a healthy and positive relationship with her.

But one day, one of my sisters called me, saying that Mum wanted to talk to me.

'Yeah, so what?' I said. But I agreed to speak to her. During that phone call she tried to say something about the past, that she never understood what had happened and why I chose not to have a relationship or any communication with her. I told her I didn't want to talk about it. Instead I asked her about what it was like for her during the war. What I was really saying was that she had never told me anything about her life or the war years. I was born just after the war and I remember some big aeroplanes flying overhead when I was young. She told me about being sent to the Midlands during the war so that she would be safe. She wasn't safe and hated every minute of it.

That brief talk was probably the longest conversation I had ever had with her! I think she wanted to try and say sorry for things that had happened, particularly before she popped her clogs, but the phone battery died before anything else could be said. She hasn't phoned back.

When I became a Christian, I visited my mum and stepfather and told them that Jesus loved them. I remember my mum's face lit up and my stepfather looked really angry. I thought this was unusual, because Mum was the one who was always against God, having been mistreated by nuns as a child. My stepfather never expressed anything one way or another and yet he seemed to demonstrate anger. I didn't feel a burden to lead them to the Lord. I just needed them to know the truth. My stepfather has since died.

When I talk to people about the lack of any relationship with my mother, some have said how sorry they are. One of the neighbours I spoke to when visiting Steep, knew my mum and commented that life was too short. I agree, but not in the way she meant it. She meant life was too short for grudges or broken relationships. I meant life was too short to get involved in damaging relationships again. This isn't about forgiveness. Reconciliation means that change and effort has to happen on both sides; it has to be a two-way thing. To have a relationship with my mother would be a negative thing and not based on truth and honesty.

My mum did the best she could, but she wasn't very good at it. She never acknowledged or apologised for her violence or lack of love and care. She is the person who gave birth to me, but she was never a mother. I understand that it was hard for her: blown out by her old man, rejected when she had two kids and pregnant with a third. But she was very dysfunctional herself and made it brutal for all of us. I certainly don't feel a sense of any special responsibility towards her as a mother because I don't and never did feel like a son.

We're still quite a dysfunctional family and I've never had close relationships with my sisters or other relatives, but my life is so full already, with my relationship with God and my wife and my Christian family. I'm not interested in relationships with family members that are so costly. I'm old now. I could pop my clogs at any time and not wake up again. Why waste time on relationships that are destructive?

I've often come across people from my past, but I don't necessarily want to keep in touch with them. I've met a few old Hell's Angel gang members, but some made it clear after the last book was released that I wasn't welcome on their patch. I had seen my old mate Steve a few times, who I was with when I had the acid trip and saw God. I had led him to the Lord at the time of the mission on the Leigh Park estate. But, the last time I saw him he showed no evidence of any faith. His mum was a practising witch and he told me that he's 'into money' now. There are many like him who become Christians and for many it is a genuine commitment, as I believe it was with him. But it gets too tough for them and they drop out. Jesus explains it in the Bible as a seed that is planted on rough ground that shoots up and then is smothered, withers and dies.

My heart doesn't grieve for these guys now. I'm not interested in reaching bikers. I'm respected by bikers in prison and it gives us common ground to talk about, but God called me to work with prisoners, which I have now done for thirty-two years.

One interesting development from my past is that I'm now friends with coppers! I like the old bill now and yet, at one time, as a Hell's Angel, they were my sworn enemy. But even as a Christian I had problems with any form of authority for a long time, including probation and prison officers. I struggled with my first probation officer when I came out of Dartmoor because of what I saw as his arrogant attitude towards me. I would have loved to have punched him and I was convinced that he wanted to see how tough I really was.

God has done a lot of work in me since then to give me the right attitude towards those in authority. However, it's still only the ones who are genuine and honest and 100 per cent straight that I respect and want anything to do with. I have no time for those who lie or mislead, throw their weight around or bully people.

In the Hell's Angels' years, there were two cops that regularly dealt with us that were good guys and I had a lot of respect for them. I think that in another life (perhaps the one I have now), I would have got on really well with them. They were straight, they meant what they said and said what they meant. It doesn't get any better than that. If only they could see me now! I remember meeting a Christian police officer when I returned to Leigh Park once who said he could not believe that I was a Christian, knowing what I used to be like. At one time I would have wanted to seriously hurt him or kill him, and now we are brothers in Christ. I found that gobsmackingly amazing and very moving. I think some of them still wonder if I'm for real. Prison officers especially found it hard having an ex-con working with them for many years, until they got to know and trust me.

I was a member of the Prison Officers' Christian Fellowship and the Christian Police Association, who used my story in one of their publications to go into custody cells. In fact, they invited me to New Scotland Yard police headquarters and I even had my own car parking space. I've also been to Drummond Gate Police headquarters, speaking at an evening dinner. Police are very canny. They check you out to see if you are for real!

When I celebrated my sixtieth birthday there were several police officers, a high court judge and a few ex-cons there, so it was really strange – but also wonderful. I thought this was what heaven must be like, with the most unlikely people all together and getting on really well.

However, before I find that out, I believe that I am about to enter a new phase in my life. My current ministry is coming to an end. Where I will end up and what I will be doing next, I have yet to discover!

— CHAPTER 16 —

Here we are, Lord, use us!

Seeing so many lives changed by God over the years has been an amazing privilege. I feel excited every day waiting to see what God has for me and it's been tremendously rewarding. However, it's also been incredibly exhausting and tough, not only because of reliving my own pain each time I tell my story, but because I feel the guys' pain from their own stories. It stresses me to pieces and often moves me to tears. Some people can leave these burdens at the prison gate and forget about them when they are not at work, but I always took them home with me because I cared so much about these men. I'm now totally drained and burnt out, and I feel like I've run a great race for many years. It's now time to finish.

At the time of writing, I'm just a few months away from walking into prison for the last time. After thirty-two years of ministry, I know that I need to retire from the role of chaplain, even though in many ways it will be awful leaving and I will miss it. But I believe it would be wrong to continue because God has other plans for me. However, although I may not be walking through the prison corridors any more, I believe this book and the DVD about my life will do the walking for me and continue to give lads hope.

My wife is retiring too and we plan to recharge our batteries for a while, travel a bit and maybe do a bit of scuba diving – we

169

were taught by a prison officer! I was down the seg one day in the New Year, feeling quite angry after having a grotty Christmas.

'Well, next year I'm going to go scuba diving or something,' I grumbled at him.

'Why did you say that?' he asked, looking puzzled.

'Well, actually, it would be nice to go scuba diving. I fancy having a go at it.'

'Did you know I'm an instructor?' he said. I was blown away by that. He started teaching us both and it meant that we also socialised with other prison officers who were on the course. We are both qualified now and looking forward to doing more of it.

I still love exploring the countryside, but don't always have the energy for it that I used to have. I was once planning to go on a survival course on Dartmoor, living off the land. All I've done so far is an eight-mile walk that nearly killed me – I ended it as a sweaty blob! I climbed over a stone wall and came face to face with a large bull, who took one look at me and ran away. Thank You, Lord!

But we do plan to explore the countryside in this country and abroad, and to travel on my trike, which is a motorbike with stabilisers so I don't fall off!

I still love bikes after all these years, but I had to get to a time in my life mentally when it became just a bike and not an object of worship as it was in the Hell's Angels' days. I had all sorts of bikes back then, apart from a Harley, which is associated with the Angels because it's what the American guys have. To me they are rubbish bikes – like tractors really.

After the embarrassing episode at college with the Honda 49cc, I bought a Triumph Saint, which was, of all things, an ex-police motorbike – it still had a place where the police radio used to go on the gas tank! I also had a Yamaha chopper and a Honda VFR, which did 0–60 in 3.6 seconds.

My trike started out as a Yamaha FJR 1300 Sports Tourer, which is built to go on forever. We got it about ten years ago and have been all over on it, but when a lovely prison officer we knew in Wandsworth was killed in a bike accident, my wife didn't want to ride it again. It had only done 4,000 miles. We put it in the back garden for five years gathering rust, until I decided to get it built into a trike, which took ten months. It's now eight inches longer and five feet wider than it used to be! It's a monstrous, noisy thing and it looks really good.

My trike even got the attention of the number-one governor at Wandsworth! He started chatting to me about it one day when I was writing a report on a prisoner and talking to one of the prison officers about my trike.

'So you've got a trike?' the governor said. 'I was thinking about getting one of them.' We had a chat about it. I didn't know he even spoke to people like me; I'm just a prison chaplain. It was wonderful though.

Even though I have always loved riding fast, I realise that zooming round lanes suicidally isn't really OK for a Christian. I'm working very hard at doodling around now and staying within the speed laws. And now any bike I own is just a bike. I don't sit around for hours polishing it to make it pretty, often to the detriment of various bikes which have got pretty grotty.

Another big change in our lives is that we're finally moving out of London – somewhere I never wanted to live in the first place. Yet we've been blessed here with a lovely God-given home with a large garden, just up the road from the countryside. In fact, when we first moved here, we used to sneak in because we were embarrassed coming into such a lovely place! I remember talking to a dear old lady at our church about this 'awfully nice middle-class church' I had spoken at and she said, 'Brian, stop saying that. You're one of us now. You're middle class.' We are part of a wonderful church where we are fed, supported and greatly blessed.

However, I would love a nice quiet house by the sea away from too many people. In fact, we've been praying for that for fifteen years.

We know that God has a new ministry for us just round the corner, which we believe could be with hurting people, including those who have been hurt by the Church. In fact, we seem to come across people like that everywhere. I remember once during a boating holiday on the Norfolk Broads, we got chatting to the guy who helped us moor up.

'I used to be a police officer,' he said.

'I used to be a villain,' I told him.

'You're Brian Greenaway, aren't you?'

He went on to tell me that he was a Christian and when he got remarried at church, everyone was angry with him, kicked him out of the church and he lost his faith. I said almost jokingly: 'Well, that's why God sent us up here, to talk to you!' It's happened regularly all over the place. Usually I want to be left alone on holiday and not talk about work, but sometimes God has other plans!

But that's all in God's hands. In reality, I want to do so much, but I'm an old guy now and don't really have the energy any more. However I have the best wife in the world who is a fantastic friend and we have really good fun. Together we are saying to God what we have always said: 'We're here, use us.'

After all these years as a Christian, I still find it totally fantastic and unbelievable that the God who flung stars into space walks with me. I don't really know what's round the corner or where we will end up next, but I'm excited by the prospect of a new direction and the tremendous privilege of continuing to serve such a wonderful God.

A life-changing decision

We all sin in our lives. Sin is everything from telling fibs, losing our temper, saying things that hurt people or physically hurting them through fights and violence. The Bible tells us that we all fall short of God's requirements. Nobody gets it right all the time and it's pointless saying things like: 'Yes I sin, but not as badly as those in prison.' You have still sinned. And if you do a lot of good things and have a good heart and care about others, that won't get you into heaven either. You still fall short! God, who is perfect, wants us to walk in His light and to know His love. Yet when we get anything wrong, immediately that sin forms a barrier like a brick wall between us and God.

The Bible tells us in John's Gospel: 'For God so loved the world that he gave his one and only Son, that whoever believes in him shall not perish but have eternal life. For God did not send his Son into the world to condemn the world, but to save the world through him. Whoever believes in him is not condemned, but whoever does not believe stands condemned already because he has not believed in the name of God's one and only Son' (John 3:16–18).

We sin in thought, word and deed, both in what we do and in what we could do and don't do. Paul, that wonderful man of God from the Bible, said in Romans: 'I do not understand what I do. For what I want to do I do not do, but what I hate I do. And if I do what I do not want to do, I agree that the law is good. As it is, it is no longer I myself who do it, but it is sin living in me. I know that nothing good lives in me, that is, in my sinful nature. For I have the desire to do what is good, but I cannot carry it out. For what I do is not the good I want to do; no, the evil I do not want to do – this I keep on doing.' (Romans 7:15–19)

God's first commandment from the Bible is that we love Him first before anything or anyone. He is a jealous God and wants us to put Him first in our lives.

If anyone thinks that a prisoner has nothing to give to society, then we have to remember that Paul was also a prisoner and hated by the religious people in his time. Paul wrote the New Testament books of Romans, 1 and 2 Corinthians, Galatians, Ephesians, Philippians, Colossians, 1 and 2 Thessalonians, 1 and 2 Timothy, Titus and possibly Hebrews. If prisoners have nothing to give to the Church, we have to throw out half of our New Testament! And of course Jesus was a prisoner. He is able to identify with prisoners because He went through a joke of a trial, before the greatest, most powerful men and highest law in the known world at that time. He was found innocent, yet taken out and whipped and finally murdered on a cross, ordered by the religious leaders of the time, who no doubt believed that they were good people.

Jesus tells us that our attitude should be to care for the prisoner as though we were in prison with them, and it is not just prisoners behind bars. Many who appear to be free are still stuck in their own prison in their lives, which is anything that traps and controls them.

The truth is that God loves you with unconditional love, not because of any good things you do, but because He is God and God is Love. And Jesus was willing to pay the ultimate price for our sins with the blood sacrifice before God when He died on that cross. This means that all who are guilty can be saved because He paid the ransom for me and you. Through Him we are restored. Isn't that something amazing, something wonderful? Though we carry so many hurts and pains, when God is involved in our everyday living, it becomes something very different and blessed.

Paul, again in the New Testament, says that in Christ Jesus we are 'a new creation; the old has gone and the new has come!' (2 Cor. 5:17). That pain, that hurt is in His hands and wherever we walk, whatever we do, He will work with us, so that His Word will be seen as true. In Him we have been born again and given a new start.

So to you who are broken, hurting and rejected, do not fear the judgment of those in the world and certainly not of the Church. We are to be judged by the perfect, all-knowing, all-loving Judge.

If through reading this book you are able to recognise that you have a need of God in your life, just ask Him to come to you (we call it praying) and say to Him: 'Lord, I am so sorry I have got so much wrong, and looking back in my life I see where I have failed so many times. Please come into my life, forgive me for all that I have done wrong and help me to be that person You want me to be. Amen.'

And for those of you who are walking with the Lord, why not ask Him today to give you the health and strength and courage to do what He wants you to do, to be the person that He wants you to be and to be in the place where He wants you to serve?

Bless you.

Brian Greenaway
the25trust@aol.com

National Distributors

UK: (and countries not listed below)
CWR, Waverley Abbey House, Waverley Lane, Farnham, Surrey GU9 8EP.
Tel: (01252) 784700 Outside UK (44) 1252 784700 Email: mail@cwr.org.uk

AUSTRALIA: KI Entertainment, Unit 21 317-321 Woodpark Road, Smithfield,
New South Wales 2164. Tel: 1 800 850 777 Fax: 02 9604 3699
Email: sales@kientertainment.com.au

CANADA: David C Cook Distribution Canada, PO Box 98, 55 Woodslee Avenue,
Paris, Ontario N3L 3E5. Tel: 1800 263 2664
Email: sandi.swanson@davidccook.ca

GHANA: Challenge Enterprises of Ghana, PO Box 5723, Accra.
Tel: (021) 222437/223249 Fax: (021) 226227 Email: ceg@africaonline.com.gh

HONG KONG: Cross Communications Ltd, 1/F, 562A Nathan Road, Kowloon.
Tel: 2780 1188 Fax: 2770 6229 Email: cross@crosshk.com

INDIA: Crystal Communications, 10-3-18/4/1, East Marredpalli,
Secunderabad – 500026, Andhra Pradesh. Tel/Fax: (040) 27737145
Email: crystal_edwj@rediffmail.com

KENYA: Keswick Books and Gifts Ltd, PO Box 10242-00400, Nairobi.
Tel: (020) 2226047/312639 Email: sales.keswick@africaonline.co.ke

MALAYSIA: Canaanland, No. 25 Jalan PJU 1A/41B, NZX Commercial Centre,
Ara Jaya, 47301 Petaling Jaya, Selangor.
Tel: (03) 7885 0540/1/2 Fax: (03) 7885 0545 Email: info@canaanland.com.my
Salvation Publishing & Distribution Sdn Bhd, 23 Jalan SS 2/64,
47300 Petaling Jaya, Selangor. Tel: (03) 78766411/78766797
Fax: (03) 78757066/78756360 Email: info@salvationbookcentre.com

NEW ZEALAND: KI Entertainment, Unit 21 317-321 Woodpark Road, Smithfield,
New South Wales 2164, Australia. Tel: 0 800 850 777 Fax: +612 9604 3699
Email: sales@kientertainment.com.au

NIGERIA: FBFM, Helen Baugh House, 96 St Finbarr's College Road, Akoka,
Lagos. Tel: (01) 7747429/4700218/825775/827264 Email: fbfm_1@yahoo.com

PHILIPPINES: OMF Literature Inc, 776 Boni Avenue, Mandaluyong City.
Tel: (02) 531 2183 Fax: (02) 531 1960 Email: gloadlaon@omflit.com

SINGAPORE: Alby Commercial Enterprises Pte Ltd, 95 Kallang Avenue #04-00,
AIS Industrial Building, 339420. Tel: (65) 629 27238 Fax: (65) 629 27235
Email: marketing@alby.com.sg

SOUTH AFRICA: Struik Christian Books, 80 MacKenzie Street, PO Box 1144,
Cape Town 8000. Tel: (021) 462 4360 Fax: (021) 461 3612
Email: info@struikchristianmedia.co.za

SRI LANKA: Christombu Publications (Pvt) Ltd, Bartleet House, 65 Braybrooke
Place, Colombo 2. Tel: (9411) 2421073/2447665 Email: dhanad@bartleet.com

USA: David C Cook Distribution Canada, PO Box 98, 55 Woodslee Avenue,
Paris, Ontario N3L 3E5, Canada. Tel: 1800 263 2664
Email: sandi.swanson@davidccook.ca

CWR is a Registered Charity – Number 294387
CWR is a Limited Company registered in England – Registration Number 1990308

Courses and seminars

Publishing and new media

Conference facilities

Transforming lives

CWR's vision is to enable people to experience personal transformation through applying God's Word to their lives and relationships.

Our Bible-based training and resources help people around the world to:
• Grow in their walk with God
• Understand and apply Scripture to their lives
• Resource themselves and their church
• Develop pastoral care and counselling skills
• Train for leadership
• Strengthen relationships, marriage and family life and much more.

Our insightful writers provide daily Bible-reading notes and other resources for all ages, and our experienced course designers and presenters have gained an international reputation for excellence and effectiveness.

CWR's Training and Conference Centre in Surrey, England, provides excellent facilities in an idyllic setting – ideal for both learning and spiritual refreshment.

 Applying God's Word
to everyday life and relationships

CWR, Waverley Abbey House,
Waverley Lane, Farnham,
Surrey GU9 8EP, UK

Telephone: +44 (0)1252 784700
Email: info@cwr.org.uk
Website: www.cwr.org.uk

Registered Charity No 294387
Company Registration No 1990308

THE MONSTER WITHIN DVD

If you enjoyed Brian's book, you'll love this powerful complementary DVD resource.

In it, Brian tells his story with gritty realism, recounting how his conversion to Christ changed his life forever, and how he has spent the last 32 years introducing thousands of prison inmates to Jesus.

This inspiring account of God's grace will encourage and amaze you and others who watch it.

Ideal for showing to churches, small groups, youth groups – and it makes a great evangelistic tool!

Presented by Brian Greenaway
EAN: 5027957001404

To see a trailer, view the current price or place your order, visit **www.cwr.org.uk**
Also available in Christian bookshops.

Encourage a friend or relative – young or old – with daily Bible-reading notes

Every Day with Jesus
Selwyn Hughes' insightful daily devotional has half a million readers worldwide. Large-print version also available.

Cover to Cover Every Day
Thought-provoking, highly original studies by respected Bible teachers.

Life Every Day
Jeff Lucas makes the Bible relevant with his legendary passion, humour and insight.

Inspiring Women Every Day
Inspiration, insight, challenge and encouragement, written by women for women.

Mettle – for 14- to 18-year-olds
Produced jointly with Youth for Christ – the contemporary design is full colour throughout.

YP's – for 11- to 15-year-olds
Dig into God's Word with imaginative, colourful design and lively, insightful writing.

Topz – for 7- to 11-year-olds
Colourful word games, puzzles, riddles and more engage children in biblical truths.

Mettle and our notes for adults are also available as email subscriptions and eBooks.

For details, including prices, visit **www.cwr.org.uk**